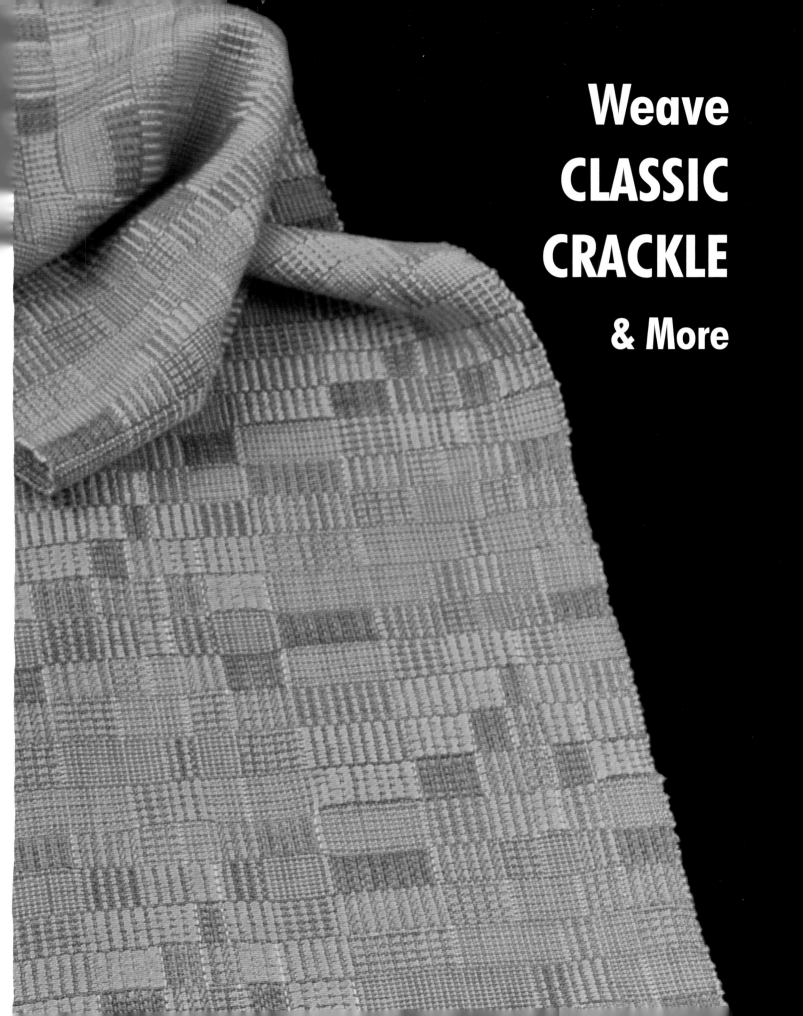

Weave
CLASSIC
CRACKLE
& More

Weave
CLASSIC
CRACKLE
& More

Susan Wilson

4880 Lower Valley Road · Atglen, PA 19310

Other Schiffer Books on Related Subjects:
Weaving Designs by Bertha Gray Hayes: Miniature Overshot Patterns, Weavers Guild of Rhode Island.
   ISBN: 9780907643-3246-3. $39.99
Tapestry Handbook: The Next Generation. Carol Russell.
   ISBN: 978-0-7643-2756-8. $59.95
Linen: From Flax Seed to Woven Cloth. Linda Heinrich.
   ISBN: 978-0-7643-3466-5. $49.99

Library of Congress Control Number: 2011929260

Type set in Futura BdCn BT/Souvenir Lt BT

ISBN: 978-0-7643-3940-0
Printed in China

Contents

Chapter 5: **More Shafts – More Blocks**

Chapter 6: **Even More with Crackle**

Acknowledgments

I was fortunate to have the assistance of three weaving colleagues, Sandy Hutton, Dottie Smith, and Mimi Smith, in reading the manuscript. Their comments and critiques have made this a better book. They helped me find those annoying little errors in drafting and numbering that tend to sneak into any writing about weaving. Any remaining errors are mine alone.

Two weave drafting software programs, *Fiberworks PCW* and *pixeLoom*, were used for drafts in the book. Many thanks to Ingrid Boesel and Bob Keates of Fiberworks and to Sue Farley of pixeLoom. Their speedy responses to my questions gave me just the help I needed for turning my drafts into images for publication.

Lucy Brusic, Bobbie Irwin, Kati Meek, Jean Scorgie, Norma Smayda, and Robyn Spady all provided invaluable advice on publishing weaving books. Nancy Schiffer, my editor at Schiffer Publishing, has provided invaluable help with the production of the book.

My husband, Bob Wilson, was so patient as I disappeared into my studio for long periods of time while working on the book. I could not have done it without his loving support.

I am deeply indebted to Mary Meigs Atwater, Harriet Tidball, and Mary Snyder, who brought crackle to American weavers in the 20th century. I feel kinship and affection for these weaving ancestors, and wish I had known them in person.

Finally, I greatly appreciate my students in crackle workshops over the last fifteen years. Your enthusiastic participation, insightful questions, and creativity in sampling have inspired me. This book is for you.

Preface

My first experience with crackle was in my college weaving class in 1969, taught by Winifred Shaw at the University of New Hampshire. By the 1970s, crackle had largely disappeared from the American handweaving world. But I was hooked. Crackle was always part of my weaving repertoire during the early years of my weaving life.

In 1986, I attended a seminar on treadling variations by Marjorie O'Shaughnessy at the Midwest Weavers Conference. That seminar was a transformative moment for me as a weaver. By that time, I had a good deal of experience with a variety of weave structures and could comfortably and independently design with them. But it had never occurred to me that one weave structure could be woven as though it were another. And then there were these special treadlings, not weave structures in themselves, that could be applied to any number of threadings. Treadling variations had been covered in various books and articles earlier in our weaving literature, but somehow my eyes had skipped past them until that seminar. I quickly started even more experimentation with crackle.

When I lived briefly in Arizona in the late 1980s, I became acquainted with Diantha States and Betty Gaudy. Both of these wonderful weavers had achieved master level Certificates of Excellence (COE) in Handweaving from the Handweavers Guild of America (HGA). Betty chose a particular design motif, the checkerboard, as the topic of her specialized study. She then examined many structures that could produce this motif. Diantha chose to do an extensive study of one structure, overshot, and various exciting ways to weave it. I was inspired by them to work on my COE. Crackle was the logical choice for the topic of my specialized study.

By the 1990s, there seemed to be a resurgence of interest in crackle by American handweavers. More articles appeared in our magazines. I was pleased to add to the literature with a few articles based on my crackle work for the COE and beyond. I began to teach weaving workshops, the first one and still the one in most in demand on crackle. And thanks to my students for their persistent requests, I have finally decided to compile what I know about crackle into a book. My intent is to have a conversation with you about crackle, as though we were having a workshop together—although I will include much more than can be covered in a two- or three-day workshop.

Chapter **1**
Introduction: Why Crackle?

A Little History

Crackle comes to us from Sweden where it is called *jämtlandsväv* or *jämtlandsdräll*, named for the area in Sweden where it apparently originated. I neither read Swedish nor have access to much Swedish weaving literature, so my account is based on the work of others, namely Mary Meigs Atwater and Mary Snyder. I have been able to examine one Swedish book on crackle, *Jämtlandsdräll* by Maria Modén-Olsson (1955), which contains 82 crackle patterns. These traditional block patterns are typically threaded on only three of the four crackle blocks and have strong rectangular design. Marguerite Davison (1944) stated that these Swedish designs appear "to have been used for both rough and smooth yarns, linens, draperies and upholsteries." To give you the flavor of Swedish *jämtlandsväv* designs, in *Figures 1-1* and *1-2* are two cloth diagrams of Modén-Olsson's drafts.

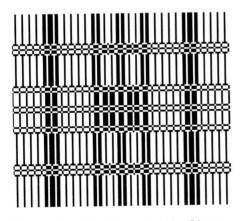

Figure I-I. Draft from Modén-Olsson (1955), page 63.

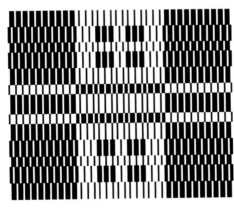

Figure I-2. Draft from Modén-Olsson (1955), page 9.

Atwater brought *jämtlandsväv* to American handweavers. Recently I have had access to a complete original set of Atwater's *Shuttle-Craft Guild Bulletins* in the Rocky Mountain Weavers' Guild reference library. Imagine my excitement when I found Atwater's very first introduction of "a Scandinavian linen weave, in the Diamond figure" in her *Bulletin* of October 1927. Atwater struggled with how to classify this "new" weave structure. In the April 1928 *Bulletin* she said this weave "is something new for four-harness weavers. It is a little pattern of a type not possible in ordinary overshot weaving," and she went on to discuss how it could be woven in the summer & winter manner. In

September 1928, Atwater offered "two more patterns distinctly 'modernistic' in character." Her first use of the name *crackle* appeared in the November 1928 *Bulletin*. But by then crackle was already a hit. She noted it was a new technique "that so many of our subscribers are using with pleasure." Later, in *Practical Weaving Suggestions* (date unknown), she commented that the Swedish name "seemed a somewhat inconvenient handle," so she gave it a

Figure 1-3.
Atwater's first draft
named crackle (1928).

new name "suggested by the texture effect which seemed to me to resemble the 'crackle' in pottery." Manuela Kaulitz (1994) further described the name crackle as referring to "crackle-glazed pottery called crackleware, itself named for *craquelure*, the fine web of cracks on old paintings." *Figure 1-3* shows a cloth diagram of Atwater's first draft officially called crackle in the November 1928 *Bulletin*.

Crackle drafts are found throughout the *Shuttle-Craft Guild Bulletins* of the 1930s and 1940s. Atwater frequently commented on the immense popularity of the weave among her members. In 1930 she said, "The more I experiment with the crackle weave, the more interesting it appears." We have a modern compilation of selected drafts from the *Bulletins* in the *Recipe Book* (1957), which was re-printed in 1969 by the Mary M. Atwater Weavers' Guild of Salt Lake City, Utah. The book is full of crackle drafts, although they are not always called crackle. Look closely at the threading of these drafts. Atwater's use of the term "modernistic" is often a code-word for crackle, and generally refers to an asymmetric block design.

Atwater certainly reflected the early twentieth century interest in modern design in her writing and crackle drafts in the *Bulletins* of that time period. In July 1929, she commented that "modernism has apparently come to stay" and that "at its best, modernistic art is extraordinarily stimulating, and —yes—beautiful. At its worst it is a cheap striving after the bizarre, quite without meaning and usually hideous." Like many of us weavers, Atwater certainly didn't hesitate to state her opinions! After further discussion of characteristics of modern design, she presented a draft for "modernistic" weaving called "Drifting Shadows," with a gently undulating, asymmetric arrangement of crackle blocks. *Figure 1-4* is a cloth diagram of that draft.

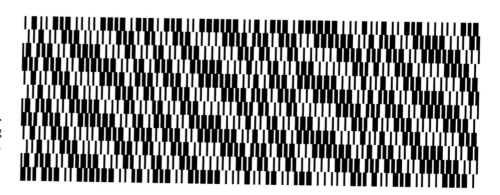

Figure 1-4.
Atwater's "Drifting
Shadows" (1929).

From 1946, Harriet Tidball continued Atwater's work with the *Shuttle-Craft Guild Bulletin* and promoted crackle in her books. Writing as Harriet Douglas, Tidball standardized crackle drafting in her *Handweaver's Instruction Manual* of 1949. She wrote, "The Scandinavian use of this technique is almost altogether for producing symmetrical, geometric patterns. Modern interpretations of the weave use simple block arrangements with emphasis on movement of areas and interesting texture variations." A profile draft of a Tidball design in the March 1949 *Bulletin* is shown in *Figure 1-5*.

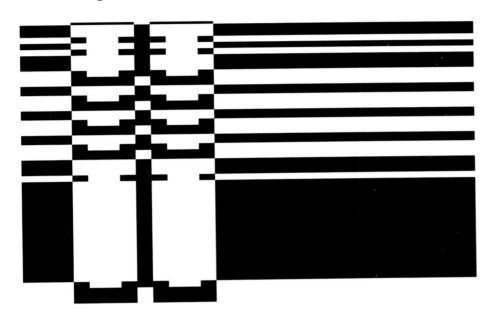

Figure 1-5.
Profile drawdown from Tidball (as Douglas, 1949).

Davison (1944) included a chapter of crackle drafts in her book, *A Handweaver's Pattern Book*, that has become a standard for 4-shaft weaving. Many of these drafts are traditional Swedish designs or derivations of overshot patterns. In 1961, Snyder published *The Crackle Weave*, the only book exclusively on crackle, a study course organized like a workshop. Snyder appears to be the first to introduce multi-shaft crackle to American handweavers, noting "there is not too much written on this." *Figure 1-6* shows a cloth diagram of an 8-shaft design from Snyder's book.

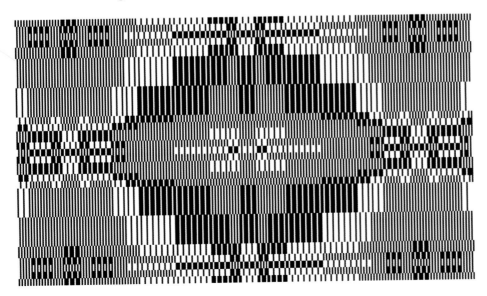

Figure 1-6.
8-shaft design from Snyder (1961), page 55.

Why Crackle?

If they included crackle at all, most authors of weaving textbooks described it positively. In her 1940s bulletins called *Handweaving News,* Nellie Sargent Johnson wrote that crackle designs "have always been popular...probably due to the fact that they are adaptable to modern effects, and also offer much variety in the weaving." Tidball (1961) discussed crackle's value for color blending and the design advantage of large blocks. For modernistic designs, she recommended arranging blocks in a profile drawdown and using that diagram for weaving, as it can be "easily copied by eye...The blocks are always so large and stylized that there is no difficulty in using this visual method, while following written directions is slow, subject to error, and unimaginative." Osma Gallinger Tod (1964) stated that "crackle is considered a very practical variation of the four-harness weaves," that it "produces a fabric of excellent wearing qualities," and is "particularly effective for rugs." S. A. Zielinski (1981) said, "From the point of view of traditional, conservative weaving, crackle is one of the best weaves for a four harness-frame loom ever invented...when explored to its limits, crackle has untold possibilities."

Other writers were less enthusiastic about crackle. Rupert Peters (1957) noted that "many weavers fear crackle" and that crackle drafting is "a nightmare." Fear? A nightmare? Berta Frey (1958) called crackle fabrics "homely" and "out of step with modern styles. The patterns have a tendency to sprawl all over the place and to look 'busy.'" Homely? Out of step? In *The Shuttle-Craft Book of American Hand-Weaving* (1928), even Atwater said of crackle, "the weave is, in a way, a makeshift weave and includes some rather troublesome eccentricities, as makeshifts are apt to do, but for all that it is a handsome and useful weave..." Makeshift? Troublesome eccentricities? By the 1970s crackle seemed to be falling out of favor with American weavers. Were they scared off by these comments? I find them challenging! Just what is so difficult about crackle? And why were Atwater's followers so enamored with it?

My aim with this book is to make crackle accessible to you. Understanding crackle is really not difficult at all. In Chapter 2, we'll look at crackle's structure, how to weave classic crackle, and how to create your own crackle designs. Then you will learn just how flexible crackle can be when we explore treadling variations in Chapter 3. Polychrome is very exciting on crackle, so I have devoted Chapter 4 to polychrome treadlings. In Chapter 5 we'll move on to weaving crackle on more shafts. You will see that we have more blocks plus something else, when we work with more shafts. I have included some other manipulations of crackle that you might find interesting in Chapter 6. I hope you find crackle as versatile and useful as I do.

Chapter **2**
Designing in Classic Crackle

Characteristics of Crackle

Crackle is a twill-based block weave. Blocks are composed of repeats of 3-shaft point twills. The number of blocks possible equals the number of shafts available. With four shafts, you can have four blocks; with eight shafts, eight blocks. We'll concentrate on four blocks now. Chapter 5 explores what happens when you work with more shafts and more blocks.

Unlike the blocks in unit weaves such as summer & winter or Bronson lace, crackle blocks are not independent of each other because they share pattern shafts in common. Crackle is not a unit weave. So when you weave for pattern in one block, you will also get pattern in an adjacent block in the A-B-C-D block order. Block B weaves pattern when you weave for pattern in Block A, Block C accompanies Block B, D comes along with C, and A with D. The remaining two blocks will be background blocks. We cannot manipulate crackle blocks independently in order to make one block of pattern and three blocks of background, or three blocks of pattern and one block of background.

There are no warp floats or weft floats longer than three ends or picks. In pattern blocks, the pattern wefts float over three warps and under one warp. Pattern wefts stack up in columns. In background blocks, the pattern wefts float under three warps and over one warp.

Crackle shares some characteristics with overshot, which is another twill-based block weave familiar to many weavers for its use in coverlets. Both crackle and overshot can produce four blocks with four shafts. But overshot's pattern weft floats travel across the entire width of the block, which can limit the practical width of the blocks. Crackle's blocks are unlimited in width. On the other hand, crackle designs tend to be larger in scale with a "blockier" look than the more delicate overshot motifs.

When compared with another familiar block weave, summer & winter, crackle has the advantage of four blocks on four shafts; summer & winter requires six shafts for four blocks. There are ways to tease the *appearance* of eight blocks of crackle on just four shafts, but for now we are just considering crackle designed in the usual manner. In Chapter 6 we'll look at a way to get the appearance of eight crackle blocks with only four shafts.

Crackle and summer & winter are similar structurally, in that pattern wefts float over three warps and under one, or over one warp and under three. Summer & winter can be woven so that its pattern wefts stack up in columns just like crackle's. But remember that crackle blocks cannot be manipulated independently as can summer & winter blocks. At the join of two adjacent crackle blocks, the pattern weft float is two ends long, giving the appearance of a slightly narrower column at that location. This effect may or may not be pleasing. In contrast, adjacent summer & winter pattern blocks maintain the three-end float and equal column width at the join.

Understanding Crackle Drafting

Block weaves create a design by an arrangement of rectangles or squares. Blocks can be any width or height, restricted in some cases (as noted above for overshot) by the fabric structure.

In order to thread a block weave we need to know a sequence of warp ends, called a *threading key*, which can be repeated over and over to make a block as wide as we want it to be. Each block in a particular weave structure has its own threading key.

Likewise, each block has its own *treadling key*, which is repeated to weave the block to the desired height.

Crackle threading keys. Crackle blocks are composed of 3-shaft point twill keys. There are a variety of ways to make 3-shaft point twills on four shafts. The points can move upward or downward. The 3-shaft keys can start at different places in the sequence. They can be written and read left to right or right to left. Swedish references usually have the points down, perhaps because European weavers often consider Shaft 1 to be at the top of the threading draft, and Shaft 4 at the bottom. In Atwater's early introduction of crackle to North American handweavers in the 1920s and 1930s, her threading keys were rather variable. In the 1950s and 1960s Tidball standardized the threading keys and Snyder followed, and these are the keys American weavers use today. They are read from right to left, and the points move upward:

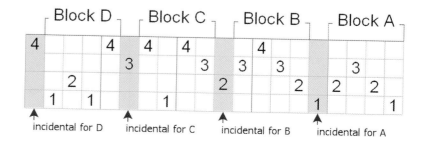

Crackle is a twill structure, and to maintain its structural integrity, twill threading conventions are used. The odd-even progression of warp ends is maintained by the addition of extra warps, called *incidentals*. Perhaps these incidentals are one of those "troublesome eccentricities" that Atwater (1928) referred to in the *Shuttle-Craft Book of American Handweaving*. But they really aren't troublesome when you follow a couple of simple rules. **First, when you finish repeating a threading key for the desired block width, finish the block with one extra end, an incidental, on the same shaft that started the block:**

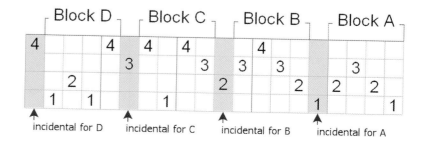

Think of this incidental, indicated by the arrows above, as the period at the end of the sentence. Once that sentence, or block, is complete with its incidental, you can move on to threading another block. If you move to an adjacent block in the A-B-C-D block order, just begin threading that block, and finish with its incidental. You'll see that the odd-even progression is maintained. Note that the point twill threading (including the incidental) within each block is completely symmetrical.

What if you want to thread your blocks in non-consecutive, or broken, order? You can certainly arrange your blocks in whatever order is called for in your design. **You'll need to thread an extra incidental between non-consecutive blocks in order to preserve the odd-even progression.** Think of that extra incidental as representing the skipped block. For example, to thread Block A followed by Block C, add either the incidental for Block B or Block D. You can choose either incidental.

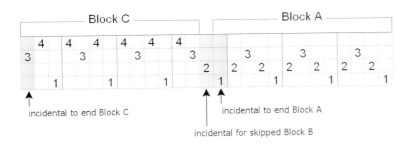

If your crackle block arrangement forms a motif with reflection symmetry, and has a broken block order on each side of the motif, choose the same incidental to use as the extra incidental on both sides of the motif. Otherwise, your motif will not look symmetrical.

For example, the center motif in *Figures 2-1* and *2-2* is created with Blocks C, D, and C. The block on either side of the motif, in the corners, is Block A, which is non-consecutive to Block C in the A-B-C-D order. You can choose either the incidental for Block B or Block D for your extra incidental to preserve the odd-even threading progression. *Figure 2-1* shows what happens to the motif if a different incidental is used on each side. In *Figure 2-2*, the same incidental, representing skipped Block B, has been used on each side. Symmetry is improved in that cloth diagram.

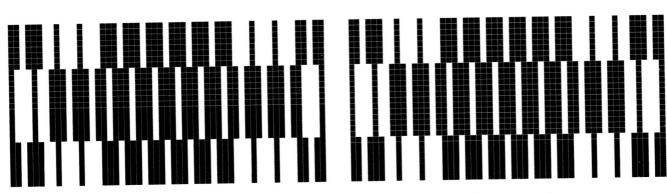

Figure 2-1. Different incidentals each side.   **Figure 2-2.** Same incidental both sides.

Can you skip both the block's ending incidental and the extra incidental when threading non-consecutive blocks?

No.

Although the odd-even progression would be preserved in the threading, there will be 4-end weft floats at the transition between blocks. True crackle does not have any floats longer than three ends. Note the 4-end pattern weft floats in the black pattern column on the right side of the center motif in *Figure 2-3*. For comparison, the column on the left side of the motif in *2-3* uses the same threading as in *Figure 2-2*, and float length of three ends is correct.

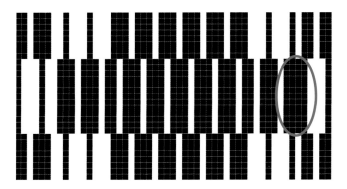

Figure 2-3. Incorrect float length of four ends.

Incidentals really are not complicated. Just follow the rules of one incidental to end the block and an extra incidental to represent a skipped block. That way you'll always be sure where your blocks begin and end.

The tie-up. Crackle is woven with a standard 2/2 twill tie-up. The ratio 2/2 expresses a twill tie-up in abbreviated form. The number on top refers to the number of shafts that are lifted. The bottom number indicates the number of shafts that are down. The total of both numbers equals the total number of shafts being used in the draft.

There are only three possible 4-shaft twill ratios: 2/2, 3/1, and 1/3. In Chapter 5 you'll see how valuable ratios are as a tool for designing tie-ups for more than four shafts.

To tie up your loom from a 2/2 ratio, tie the first pattern treadle based on the ratio, the first two shafts tied and the other two shafts not tied. The next pattern treadle follows the same ratio, but starts the tying sequence one shaft up from the preceding treadle.

Crackle's tie-up is:

4	4				4
3				3	3
		2	2		2
	1	1		1	
1	2	3	4	a	b

This tie-up is for a rising shed loom. If you are using a sinking shed loom, simply tie the spaces rather than the numbers. Six treadles give us four pattern treadles, labeled *1*, *2*, *3*, and *4*, and two tabby treadles, labeled *a* and *b*. In order to ensure your pattern blocks appear where they should, be sure to tie up and label your pattern treadles exactly as shown. Because crackle is a twill-based weave, tabby treadles tie odd shafts *vs.* even shafts. Your tabby treadles can be placed together on the right, left, middle, or one on each side of the pattern treadles, whichever is most comfortable for you. Just be sure that the tabby treadle labeled *a* ties up shafts 1-3, and *b* ties up 2-4. This will be particularly important later when we explore other treadling methods on crackle.

Treadling classic crackle. Crackle is most commonly woven in the manner of overshot, pattern alternating with tabby. Traditional Swedish *jämtlandsväv* and most of Atwater's designs were woven this way. In fact, the overshot treadling method is often the only one given in weaving texts. But Tidball (1961) noted "the classic crackle method omits the tabby and follows the rhythm of the draft with the use of three shuttles, each carrying a different color of thread... The chief design advantage is beautiful color blendings and gentle movement of the dominant color from block to block according to the pattern the weaver desires." When I read this, my curiosity was piqued! Classic crackle became the foundation for my exploration of crackle for the HGA Certificate of Excellence in Handweaving.

Classic crackle is woven exactly as drawn in, including an incidental to complete each block and to represent any skipped blocks. Using the standard 2/2 twill tie-up, with pattern treadles numbered as above, the block treadling keys (read from top down) for classic crackle are:

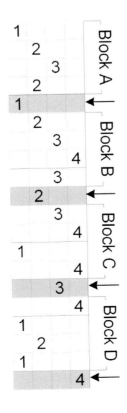

Tabby treadles are not used in classic crackle. Incidentals are indicated by arrows.

Pattern treadle numbers in the treadling keys correspond with shaft numbers in the threading keys. For example, Block A is threaded [1-2-3-2] and is treadled [1-2-3-2]. When you treadle for pattern in one block, you will also get pattern in the next block in the twill order. Treadling keys are 3-pick point twills, just as in threading. Twill structure is maintained with incidentals at the end of blocks (like the period at the end of the sentence) *and* for skipped blocks, just the same as in the threading.

Another way to express the treadling keys, which I will use throughout the rest of the book, is by treadle number or letter in a horizontal chart format:

Block A:	1 (ground x)	2 (pattern)	3 (ground y)	2 (pattern)
Block B:	2 (ground x)	3 (pattern)	4 (ground y)	3 (pattern)
Block C:	3 (ground x)	4 (pattern)	1 (ground y)	4 (pattern)
Block D:	4 (ground x)	1 (pattern)	2 (ground y)	1 (pattern)

There are three wefts: one pattern weft and two ground wefts, x and y. The pattern weft can be heavier or the same size as ground wefts.

Start the treadling sequence with ground x, then pattern, then ground y, then pattern. When the block reaches the desired height, end the block with an incidental of ground x using the same treadle that started the block. Note that within the block, pattern wefts alternate with ground wefts, and the two ground wefts alternate with each other.

At the transition between blocks there are two picks of ground x next to each other but in different sheds. The color order remains the same in all four treadling keys. If you skip blocks in the treadling, you might choose to use ground y for the incidental representing the skipped block, to avoid having three picks of ground x in a row.

Managing three shuttles may seem awkward at first, but a rhythm does develop.

The Classic Crackle Structure

Classic crackle produces four distinctly different blocks. Examine the structural draft of classic crackle in *Figure 2-4* to observe some of its unique characteristics.

When you weave for pattern in one block, there is also pattern in the next block in the A-B-C-D order. The remaining two blocks are background. But, the two pattern blocks are different from each other, as are the two background blocks.

Both pattern blocks have dense 3-end pattern weft floats stacked up in columns. One pattern block will show floats of one of the ground colors. The other ground color passes over only one warp, and disappears beneath the pattern wefts in that block. The opposite color arrangement is true for the accompanying pattern block. Background blocks have 3-end floats of the ground wefts, one ground color in each block. Because each block starts and ends with ground x, there will be a solid line of the ground x color where blocks change.

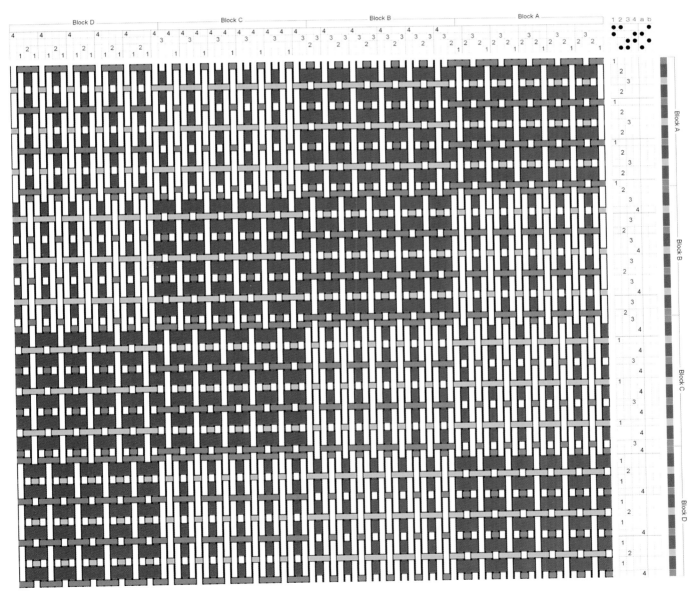

Figure 2-4. Classic crackle structural draft.

Classic crackle is entirely a twill structure; no tabby is used. Without plain weave picks to hold the warps in alignment, one of the eccentricities of classic crackle emerges. As blocks grow taller, warps tend to shift together or apart, distorting the apparent width of the columns. At the join of two background blocks, occasionally pattern wefts that should remain on the back "pooch" out to the front of the cloth. A vertical line of pattern color appears, out of place, at that spot (indicated by arrows in *Figure 2-5*). At the join of two pattern blocks, warps shift closer together, and pattern weft pooches out on the back. Atwater named the structure crackle because of its overall speckled appearance when woven in the overshot manner. But I refer to these irregular vertical "cracks" in classic crackle as the *true* crackles.

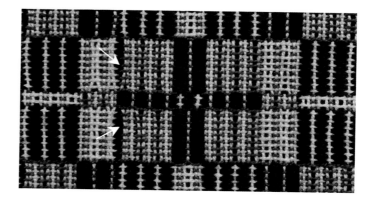

Figure 2-5. Crackles!

Unfortunately, perhaps, these crackles are neither controllable nor predictable. Changing the denting in the reed can sometimes, but not always, help minimize the occurrence of crackles. I have had them show up in warps that are sleyed one end per dent, and have not always been able to prevent them by sleying the warps closer or farther apart in places where they occur but are not wanted. They tend to appear more often with slippery yarns and less often in shorter blocks.

Because we put incidentals at the end of blocks, crackle's threading is always symmetrical within blocks. Nevertheless, the crackles do not always appear in corresponding places on each side of symmetrical block arrangements, as seen in *Figure 2-5*. A crackle might pop up on one side of a diamond, but not where you would expect in the same spot on the other side. If the crackles are distracting to the overall design, you might prefer to use other treadling methods, which we'll discuss in Chapter 3, that don't produce these crackles. On the other hand, in asymmetrical and broken block arrangements, their randomness can add interest to the cloth. Enjoy the serendipity!

Using Profile Drafts

Profile drafting is a powerful design tool for use with block weaves, including crackle. The arrangement of blocks into a motif, the proportions or relative sizes of those blocks, and the location of pattern vs. background blocks can all be determined in a profile draft. A profile draft does not indicate weave structure. It is strictly a design draft.

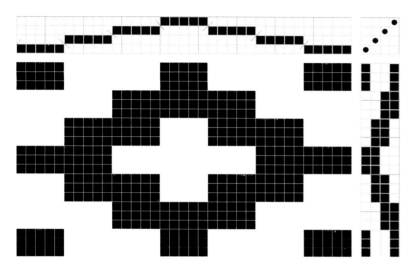

Figure 2-6. Profile draft.

A profile draft (*Figure 2-6*) is laid out in four quadrants, the same as a structural draft:
- **Upper left** (along the top) is the profile threading. Each horizontal row represents a block, starting with Block A in the bottom row. Each square in a row represents one repeat of the threading key for a particular weave structure. Incidentals are not accounted for in a profile threading. As a reminder, I usually put a diagonal hatch mark across the corner of the last square in each block. If an incidental is needed for a skipped block, I add another hatch mark.
- **Upper right** is the profile tie-up. Each single square indicates one pattern block in threading and treadling.
- **Lower right** (along the right side) is the profile treadling. Each column represents a block, starting with Block A on the left. Each square in a column represents one repeat of the treadling key for the weave structure. Again, incidentals are not depicted in a profile treadling, but need to be remembered when weaving classic crackle.
- **Lower left** (the largest area) is the profile cloth diagram which shows the overall layout of the block design. Note: Because two adjacent blocks weave pattern in crackle, I have marked pairs of squares in the treadling so that the cloth diagram depicts a crackle design.

In designing my own crackle drafts, I usually start with a profile threading to determine my block order and widths. I then move to the cloth diagram section of the profile draft and decide how I want the pattern areas to look in the cloth. Black areas represent pattern blocks; white areas are background. At this point, I often make adjustments to the placement or sizes of the blocks in the threading to get the design or motif I desire. I then derive the profile treadling from the cloth diagram. Remember that because two pattern blocks weave together, the cloth design will be chunkier in appearance than in the profile threading.

Profile drafting helps us understand and adapt crackle drafts from the many excellent sources in our weaving literature. Atwater's *Recipe Book*, Snyder's *The Crackle Weave*, and Davison's *A Handweaver's Pattern Book* are filled with interesting crackle drafts. But often it is not apparent from looking at those threadings just what the block arrangement is. It's also not always obvious, despite any markings by the author, just where a design repeat begins and ends. If a border is given, does the border end and does the block pattern begin where indicated? Not always! Identify the blocks and incidentals and make a profile threading to better visualize the layout of the blocks. You will readily see whether you need to add any extra blocks at the end to balance or complete a design.

If you want to use a draft from a reference that does not use our conventional modern block threading keys, first identify the blocks in the existing draft, using the keys provided in that reference. Then create a profile threading to depict the block order and widths. Finally, re-interpret the profile draft using our conventional threading keys. Be sure to account for the incidentals.

It is well worth the small amount of extra time and effort to make a profile draft to understand how an existing structural draft works. You can then modify the threading or treadling to create the design you want.

Design Ideas

Designing your own block layouts. Use profile drafting to create your own crackle designs or adapt existing ones. Suppose you like a motif, such as blooming leaf, from another block weave like overshot and want to weave that motif in crackle. You can borrow that motif using profile drafting. First, identify the blocks in the threading draft of the "parent" structure. Then convert to a profile threading. Now substitute crackle threading keys into your profile draft. Scale can be a concern when making conversions from overshot to crackle. Overshot blocks are composed of 2-end keys and blocks share one end in common where they join. Overshot motifs tend to be small and delicate. Crackle treadling keys are 4-end repeats, plus the extra incidental end where blocks join. Overshot designs interpreted as crackle quickly become large and blocky.

Kaulitz (1994) suggests using any twill threading draft as a profile draft for crackle. Because you are substituting four crackle ends for each single twill end, familiar twill shapes, such as diagonals, points, advancing points, and undulations, increase in scale when interpreted as crackle.

Although we have four possible blocks, we do not have to use all of them in our designs. Frey (1958) recommends using 3-block designs to make crackle "a more interesting fabric." Traditional Swedish *jämtlandsväv* patterns such as those seen in Modén-Olsson (1955) frequently have only three blocks in the threading, but all four blocks may be treadled. Likewise, you can thread an even number of blocks, but treadle an odd number. Broken block orders in threading and/or treadling can make lively designs in which the pairs of pattern blocks do not overlap, but just touch at the corners.

For an accent, an extra incidental can be threaded in the middle of a wide block. Finish the first series of repeats of the key for that block, ending with the incidental for that block. Next insert an incidental on an adjacent shaft to indicate a skipped block. Then begin the next series of repeats for the original wide block. The extra incidental will produce a single column of pattern or background, a "phantom" of the block represented by the extra incidental, adding interest in a blocky design. In the two blocks adjacent to the accent, however, two narrower columns of pattern or background appear next to each other, producing a bit of irregularity. *Figure 2-7* shows a "modernistic" or asymmetrical design from Atwater's *Recipe Book* (1969) Series V, No. 18. Compare the motifs with the extra incidental on the right side of the cloth diagram with those on the left side without an extra incidental. The black pattern and white background accent columns created by the extra incidental pose no problem structurally and do strengthen the design.

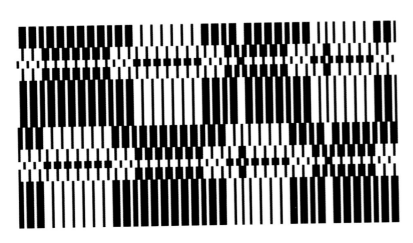

Figure 2-7.
Extra incidentals for accent on the right side of the design but not on the left.

Color and value. Classic crackle, with its warp and three wefts, has exciting potential for color work. One way to start an exploration of color is to make a gamp or sampler, as in *Figure 2-8*. A value gamp (*Figure 2-9*), using white, black, and a range of grays in between, is also a useful exercise.

We often make color gamps in plain weave and twill, but there is no reason why we can't make them in pattern weaves like crackle as well. For warp, select the three primary colors (red, yellow, blue) and three secondary colors (orange, green, violet). Add tertiary or intermediate colors if available for even more combinations. Arrange the colors in wide stripes in the warp in the order they appear in the spectrum. For simplicity, thread your crackle blocks in a straight diagonal A-B-C-D order.

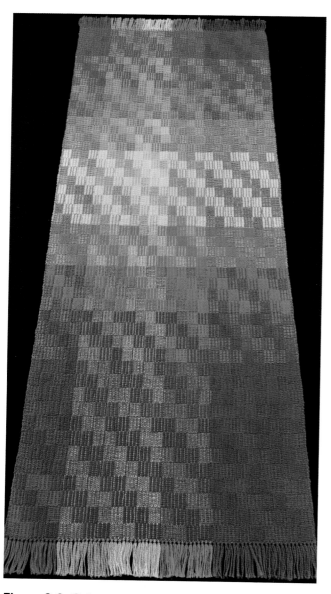

Figure 2-8. Color gamp.

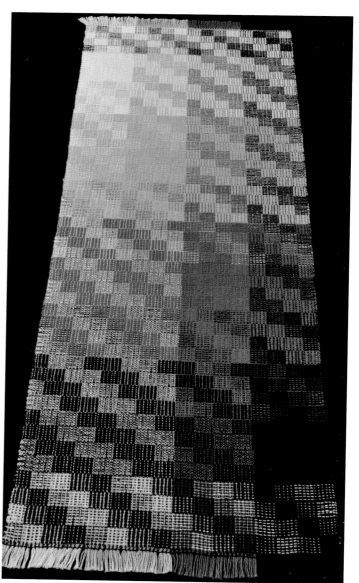

Figure 2-9. Value gamp.

There are many ways you could work with your weft colors in a classic crackle gamp. Here's one possibility. Using the first three colors of the spectrum for the three wefts, weave ground x, pattern, ground y, pattern. After you have woven four blocks with this color order, start progressing through the various combinations. Drop the color used for ground x, move the pattern color to ground x position, and ground y becomes pattern. Add the next color in the spectrum as ground y. Continue rotating through your colors until you have woven all combinations. The silk scarf in *Figure 2-10* is actually a color gamp that uses this color rotation method.

Figure 2-10. Classic crackle scarf, silk. *Yarn courtesy of Red Fish Dye Works.*

Figure 2-10a.
Detail.

Ground weft color order can make a big difference in the appearance of your design. In *Figures 2-11* and *2-12* are two samples with diamond-shaped motifs. Warp is natural cotton, pattern weft is medium blue, and ground wefts are pink and dark burgundy. One blue pattern block looks darker because floats of the burgundy ground weft blend with the blue. The other blue pattern block, with floats of pink, looks lighter. One background block is darker, dominated by burgundy floats; in the other, pink dominates. Although they look strikingly different, these samples are identical except for the ground weft designations. In *2-11*, ground weft *x* is burgundy and *y* is pink. Look for the darker line where two burgundy wefts occur together. One burgundy weft ends a block and another burgundy weft follows, starting the next block. In *2-12*, *x* is pink and *y* is burgundy. There is a less obvious pink weft line at the transition between blocks. Also note that the two ground wefts change positions in both background and pattern blocks in the two samples. In *2-11* the burgundy background block is in the center of the diamond, and the darker pattern blocks are around the outside of the diamond. In *2-12*, the opposite color arrangement occurs, pink in the center and around the outside of the diamond.

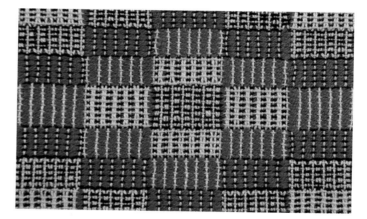

Figure 2-11. Ground weft *x* is burgundy and *y* is pink.

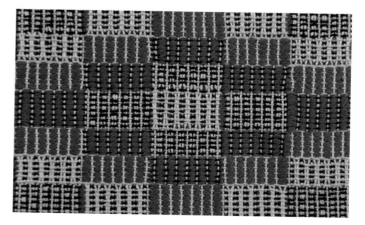

Figure 2-12. Ground weft *x* is pink and *y* is burgundy.

With small motifs and small blocks, it is generally best to establish your ground weft order and stay with it throughout the piece. Otherwise, the design can be obscured and the overall effect is busy. But with large blocks, there is more surface area in pattern and background for experimentation with changing ground weft order or colors from block to block or mid-block. In one of my workshops, Jan Towsley of Rochester, New York, did just that with large blocks threaded in the diagonal A-B-C-D order. *Figure 2-13* shows my table runner, inspired by Jan's samples. When treadled for pattern in Block A, Block B also weaves pattern. Blocks C and D are background. The two pattern blocks together look like one large block, as do the two background blocks. When treadling switches to the opposite blocks, the two pairs of pattern block touch at the corners, rather than overlapping. A checkerboard results. Look closely at the detail view in *Figure 2-13a*. When ground weft order changes mid-block, a checkerboard also appears within the pattern blocks and within the background blocks, because the large squares are actually composed of two blocks each.

Having the chance to work with four different color elements (warp and three wefts) simultaneously in crackle can be both exciting and overwhelming. You could just use one weft, but in 4-shaft crackle, the results are not particularly interesting. When we move to multi-shaft crackle in Chapter 5, you'll see that weaving classic crackle with one weft is a useful option.

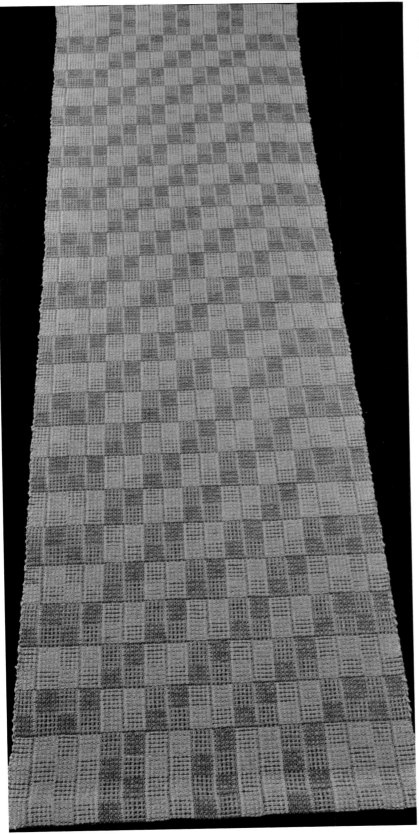

Figure 2-13. Classic crackle table runner, linen and cotton.

Figure 2-13a. Detail.

One way to get control of the colors and unify the design is to make two of the four elements (warp, pattern weft, ground *x*, ground *y*) the same color. The baby blanket in *Figure 2-14* has the same five colors in the warp and both ground wefts; pattern weft is a lightly-textured natural cotton. All of the color blending occurs in the negative spaces, the background blocks.

Figure 2-14a.
Detail.

Figure 2-14. Classic crackle baby blanket, cotton, crocheted edge.

Shown in *Figure 2-15* is a wool scarf in which the design is unified with black in both warp and pattern weft. As in the baby blanket, all the color action is in the background. Five colors of ground wefts were rotated over four blocks, two at a time, dropping one color and adding another at every block change. After 20 blocks, the color rotation starts again in the same blocks. Mixing an odd number of repeats or colors in the treadling with an even number of blocks in the threading makes a design appear more complex.

Figure 2-15.
Classic crackle scarf, wool.

Figure 2-15a.
Detail.

Making a sampler. Weaving a sampler is a good way to see how classic crackle works and learn to make your own designs. Make a warp three to five yards long, so that you also can experiment with treadling variations that follow in Chapters 3 and 4. I recommend a smooth, light-colored warp yarn at an appropriate sett for a slightly open plain weave. Classic crackle is a twill structure and generally works best sett for twill. But many of the other treadling variations that follow need a more open sett. For sampling, a compromise is in order. 10/2 mercerized cotton at 20 e.p.i. is a good choice.

Plan a block arrangement that will be about 160 ends, or eight inches, wide. I suggest simple block orders, such as diagonal, point, or zigzag, with no blocks narrower than about ½ inch. That way you'll be able to easily identify your blocks as you weave. Use profile drafting as your design tool for laying out your blocks. Don't forget the incidentals!

Choose a pattern weft that is slightly heavier than the warp. 5/2 cotton works well if 10/2 is used in the warp. The two ground wefts should be the same size as the warp. In future classic crackle projects you may prefer that warp and wefts are all the same weight; adjust sett accordingly. In your sampler, all three of the wefts should be very different in color and value from each other and the warp. You will want to be able to see clearly how each yarn performs. Sometimes color combinations that seem the most unlikely yield the most exciting samples.

For your first sample, repeat the treadling key for Block A until the block is about three-quarters of an inch tall. Then weave Block B for ¾ inch, followed by C and D. Keep your wefts in the same order in each block, always starting and ending the block with ground x. You will now have a woven profile that shows you where your blocks are. These are your design elements. Next, determine a block treadling order to use throughout the rest of the sampler. I recommend designing a motif, such as a diamond, that will be easily recognized in each of our many treadling variations. Keep the design simple, with no blocks shorter than about ½ inch. Weave a classic crackle sample or two in your motif. You'll then be ready to try some of the other ways of weaving crackle to come.

Chapter 3
Versatile Crackle: Treadling Variations

Crackle may indeed be a "makeshift weave," as described by Mary Atwater. Blocks are not independent of each other, but share ends in common. Incidentals are needed to maintain the integrity of the twill structure. But this makeshift nature may be what gives crackle its superb flexibility. As we have seen in Chapter 2, classic crackle produces some fascinating effects. Many interesting variations can be obtained when crackle is woven in the manner of other weave structures or by using special treadling methods. There is no law that says we have to weave any structure only in its traditional way!

Treadling in the Manner of Other Weaves

Your loom is threaded and tied-up for crackle, but let's see what happens if you pretend it's threaded to some other structure and weave it as if it were that structure. Some surprising and useful fabrics result.

Crackle woven as twill. As we might expect, because crackle is a twill-based weave, twill treadlings are very successful on crackle. When treadled as straight twill [1-2-3-4] using just the pattern treadles in our standard 2/2 tie-up, the point twill structure of the blocks is evident. Examine *Figure 3-1*. You can almost read the threading by simply examining the cloth. A contrasting weft shows the structure more clearly. Yarn choices, sett, and beat all influence how well the points show. Try using a tabby in the same color as the warp alternating with the twill wefts to open up the twill pattern if needed.

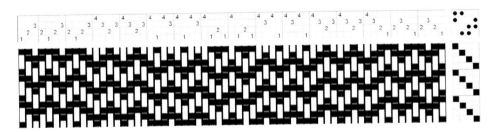

Figure 3-1. Treadled as straight twill.

Point or reverse twill treadling order, as well as extended point twill treadlings such as rosepath or goose *eye*, "M and W" twill, or advancing twill, are also effective. Examples of these twill treadlings are shown in *Figures 3-2, 3-3, 3-4*, and *3-5*. Crackle blocks are threaded in a point arrangement in these examples.

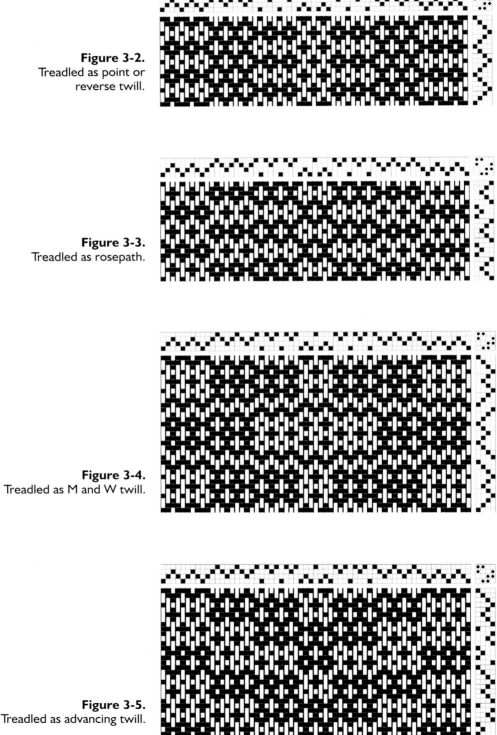

Figure 3-2.
Treadled as point or reverse twill.

Figure 3-3.
Treadled as rosepath.

Figure 3-4.
Treadled as M and W twill.

Figure 3-5.
Treadled as advancing twill.

Crackle woven as overshot. The overshot treadling method is the most common and most traditional way of weaving crackle. Swedish *jämtlandsväv* was woven this way, and often this is the only method discussed in modern references.

For the overshot treadling and almost all of the other treadling variations in this chapter, we'll use the standard 2/2 tie-up discussed in Chapter 2:

4	4				4
3				3	3
		2	2		2
	1	1		1	
1	2	3	4	a	b

Pattern treadles are labeled *1, 2, 3,* and *4.* Tabby treadles are labeled *a* and *b.* I'll use these numbers and letters for all the block treadling keys that follow.

Like crackle, overshot is a twill-based block weave, with four blocks possible on four shafts. Traditional overshot is woven with two wefts, pattern and tabby. Pattern wefts are typically a bit heavier than the warp and contrasting in color. Tabby wefts usually are the same color and size as warp. Pattern and tabby alternate until the block is as tall as desired. Tabby *a* and tabby *b* alternate to create a plain weave ground cloth. Pattern wefts are supplementary, floating over or under groups of warps, to create a design of pattern, half-tone, and plain weave background areas.

Much has been written about treadling variations on overshot threadings, and you'll find a number of good references in the Bibliography at the end of this book. Because crackle and overshot are so closely related, these overshot treadling variations can almost always be applied directly to a crackle threading. Block treadling keys will be identical, although the block labels may shift. For example, a treadling key for pattern in Block B in overshot may actually produce pattern in Block A in crackle.

When crackle is woven as overshot, shown in *Figure 3-6,* two blocks weave as pattern and two as background. Note that pattern Treadle 1 makes

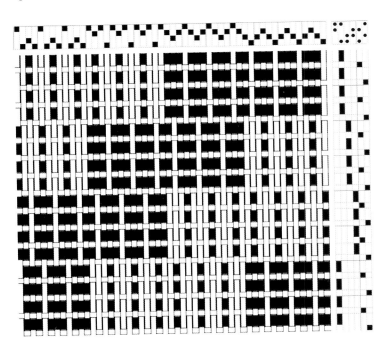

Figure 3-6.
Treadled as overshot.

pattern in Block D, but also in the adjacent Block A. Likewise, Treadle 2 produces pattern in Block A and also in Block B, and so on. The block treadling keys for treadling in the overshot manner are:

Block A (and also B):	2 a 2 b
Block B (and also C):	3 a 3 b
Block C (and also D):	4 a 4 b
Block D (and also A):	1 a 1 b

Pattern wefts stack up in columns as they float over three warps and under one in the pattern blocks. Where two adjacent pattern blocks join, the column is noticeably narrower, as it is only two warps wide. Background blocks show wider columns of the plain weave ground cloth and vertical lines composed of dots of pattern color. In the background areas pattern wefts float under three warps and over one, with narrower background columns at the join between adjacent blocks. In this draft, black pattern wefts are twice as thick as white tabby wefts.

Crackle woven as overshot produces a sturdy, smooth fabric with strong pattern blocks. The plain weave ground cloth holds warps and wefts on the grid, so there are no unpredictable "crackles" to disturb symmetry. Traditional crackle designs tend to have light background with dark pattern. In *Figure 3-7* a traditional diamond crackle motif is shown woven as overshot. You'll see this motif again throughout this chapter illustrating other treadling methods. Here is a profile threading of the diamond motif:

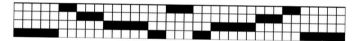

In these diamond samples, warp and tabby wefts are 10/2 natural mercerized cotton; pattern wefts are 3/12 worsted wool.

Overshot treadling does afford an opportunity for color and texture experimentation. The strong blocks hold up well with textured pattern yarns. Space-dyed yarns can work as either pattern or tabby wefts, although the pattern may be lost if there is wide range of values in the colors of the space-dyed yarn. Stripes are effective in the warp. You might change colors where the blocks change or blend colors within blocks across the warp. Pattern wefts can be the same size as warp and tabby wefts, or slightly larger.

Figure 3-7.
Sample woven
in the manner of
overshot.

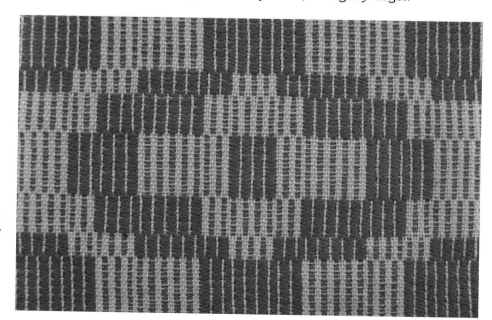

In *Figures 3-8* and *3-9* are two towel fabrics adapted from Atwater's *Recipe Book*, Series V No. 22. *Figure 3-8* illustrates a traditional interpretation of the design. The towel in *Figure 3-9* has a warp of wide stripes; colors change where the motif changes. Variegated yarn is used in *every* other stripe section, and two solid colors alternate with each other and the variegated stripes. The two solid warp colors also alternate as tabby, each used for the height of one motif. The dark blue pattern weft forms the pattern on a colorful ground.

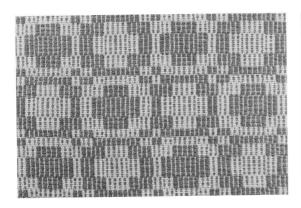

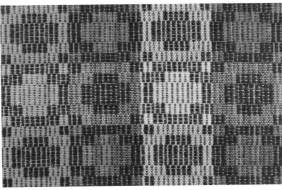

Far left:
Figure 3-8. Towel fabric, cotton, solid color warp.

Left:
Figure 3-9. Towel fabric, cotton, multi-color striped warp.

The silk scarf with a striped warp in *Figure 3-10* has a lively, contemporary look. Blocks of varying widths and heights are both threaded and treadled in straight A-B-C-D order, producing a diagonal motif. Each warp stripe is a solid color the width of a single block. The pearl gray pattern weft is lighter in value than any of the warp colors, and the tabby weft is a medium value gray that "disappears" into the multi-color warp stripes.

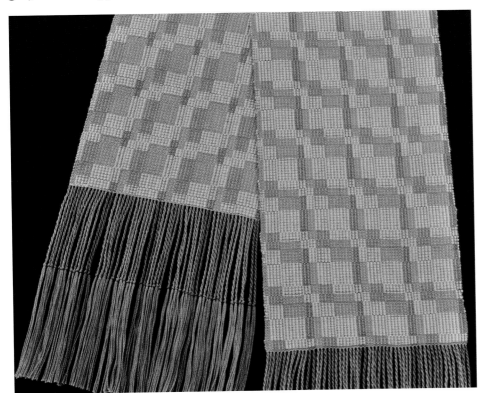

Figure 3-10. Scarf, silk, woven in the overshot manner.

Figure 3-10a. Detail.

Crackle woven as summer & winter. Summer & winter is a tied block weave that produces two blocks on four shafts. Blocks are independent of each other, so that one block can weave pattern and the other background, both can weave pattern, or both background. Like overshot, summer & winter is woven pattern alternating with tabby. The plain weave ground cloth has a supplementary pattern weft floating over three warps and under one in pattern blocks and under three-over one in background blocks.

Clotilde Barrett (1979) identifies seven traditional ways to weave summer & winter that result in three basic effects. Pattern wefts can stack up in columns, they can be staggered as in bricks, and they can be paired together but also arranged as bricks. Columns are produced by using only one of the ties in the block treadling keys. This method is sometimes called "half-dukagang," and is the same as treadling in the overshot manner. Bricks result when the two ties are alternated in treadling the pattern picks; often this method is referred to as "single" summer & winter. When the ties are paired and then alternated, as in 1-1-2-2, pattern wefts are arranged as paired bricks, often called "paired" summer & winter.

In summer & winter tie-ups there are two pattern treadles for each block or combination or blocks. One treadle operates the tie on Shaft 1, the other the tie on Shaft 2. In treadling crackle as summer & winter we use our standard twill tie-up, but weave the blocks in the same manner as we would for summer & winter, using two adjacent pattern treadles for each block. The eight-pick block treadling keys for treadling crackle as summer & winter are:

Paired bricks		**Single bricks**	
Block A:	2 a 1 b 1 a 2 b	Block A:	1 a 2 b 1 a 2 b
Block B:	3 a 2 b 2 a 3 b	Block B:	2 a 3 b 2 a 3 b
Block C:	4 a 3 b 3 a 4 b	Block C:	3 a 4 b 3 a 4 b
Block D:	1 a 4 b 4 a 1 b	Block D:	4 a 1 b 4 a 1 b

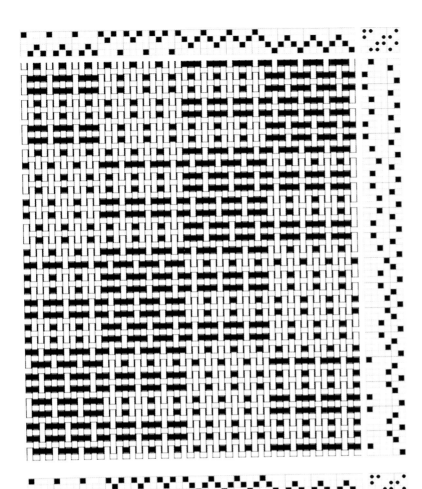

Treadling crackle as paired or single summer & winter produces some surprises. No longer do we have two pattern blocks and two background blocks. Instead, there is one pattern block, structurally identical to a summer & winter pattern block. There is one background block, structurally identical to a summer & winter background block. The background block is the *opposite* (or non-adjacent in the A-B-C-D block order) block to the pattern block. And then there are two intermediate or half-tone blocks, in the two adjacent blocks, in between the pattern and background blocks. The structural draft in *Figure 3-11* illustrates paired summer & winter treadling on crackle. *Figure 3-12* shows single summer & winter treadling.

Figure 3-11.
Treadled as paired summer & winter.

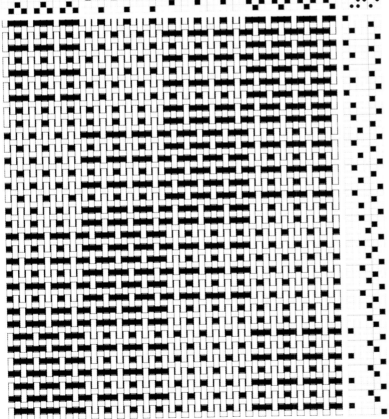

Figure 3-12.
Treadled as single summer & winter.

There are often idiosyncrasies when we apply a treadling for one weave structure to the threading of a different structure. Direct translation doesn't always work. You may need to sit at your loom and experiment to find a way to weave an attractive and useful fabric that captures the spirit of the borrowed treadling. In the case of single summer & winter treadling on crackle, you may have noticed that when you are ascending the block order, A to D, there are two pattern picks in the same shed, although separated by a tabby, when you move from one block to another. This does not occur in the descending block order. Sometimes these two pattern picks are a distraction in the finished cloth, other times not. You might avoid this effect by reversing the pattern pick order in alternate blocks. For example, weave Block A as above [1-a-2-b-1-a-2-b], followed by Block B [3-a-2-b-3-a-2-b], then Block C [3-a-4-b-3-a-4-b], and Block D [1-a-4-b-1-a-4-b]. Paired treadling does not present this problem as each block begins and ends with a single, not paired, pattern pick.

Weaving crackle as summer & winter is a way to get quite complex designs with just four shafts. But, the overall look can be somewhat busy, especially in designs with small blocks. In general, choose smooth pattern wefts that contrast in value with the warp and tabby wefts the same color as the warp. Textured and variegated pattern yarns tend to obscure the design. You'll need to experiment with sett and with relative weights or grists of pattern wefts and warps to get the clearest pattern in the wet-finished cloth. *Figure 3-13* shows our diamond motif treadled paired summer & winter; *Figure 3-14* shows single summer & winter treadling.

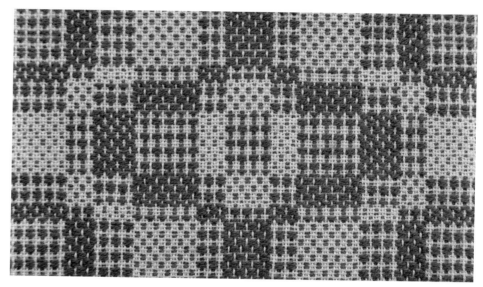

Figure 3-13.
Sample woven in the manner of paired summer & winter.

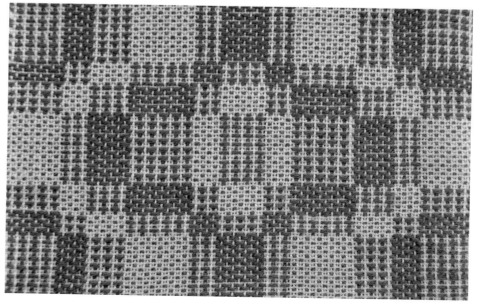

Figure 3-14.
Sample woven in the manner of single summer & winter.

The table runner in *Figure 3-15* has a traditional border pattern treadled paired summer & winter. We'll revisit this table runner later in this chapter to see how the solid white areas are treadled.

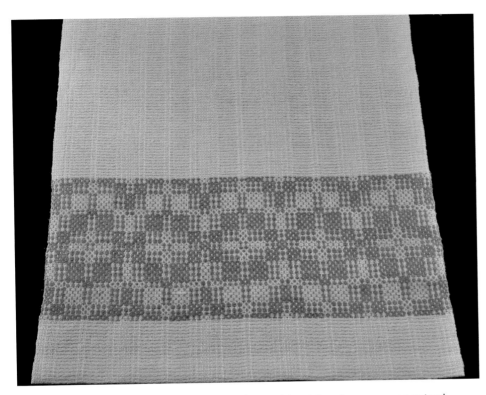

Figure 3-15. Table runner, linen and linen/rayon blend, border woven as paired summer & winter.

Crackle woven as Bronson lace. You might be tired of weaving with two or more shuttles and wish you had threaded your loom for lace. Well, you *can* make lace on a crackle threading, by weaving as if it were Bronson lace, or by using other lace treadlings we'll discuss later in this chapter.

Bronson lace is a block weave that has two blocks on four shafts. As a unit weave, Bronson lace blocks are independent of each other. You can weave one block lace and the other plain weave, both blocks lace, or both blocks plain weave. Treadling keys for Bronson lace are 6-pick repeats, with the general sequence of [a-pattern-a-pattern-a-b].

Treadling keys for crackle woven in the manner of Bronson lace are:

Block A:	a 2 a 2 a b
Block B:	a 3 a 3 a b
Block C:	a 4 a 4 a b
Block D:	a 1 a 1 a b

Crackle woven as Bronson lace, shown in the structural draft in *Figure 3-16*, produces four different lace blocks and no plain weave blocks. Some of the blocks have more warp emphasis and others more weft emphasis. None of the blocks is structurally the same as Bronson lace, so my assignment of block treadling keys is purely arbitrary. I chose the block that had the most open weft-lace look of Bronson, called that the "main" pattern block, and derived the remaining treadling keys from there. Lace is typically woven with matching warp and weft. In more complex motifs composed of small blocks, such as our diamond in *Figure 3-17*, the design can be difficult to see.

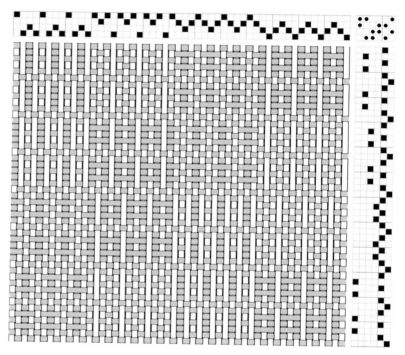

Figure 3-16.
Treadled as Bronson lace.

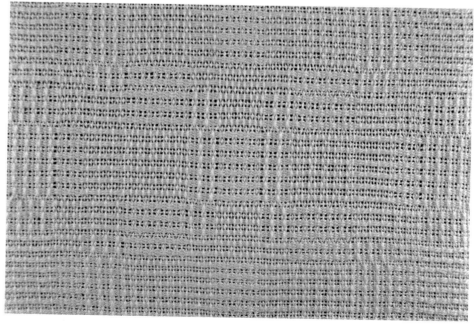

Figure 3-17.
Sample woven in the manner of Bronson lace.

For better pattern definition, try using a weft that contrasts very slightly with the warp in value. Two different colors of the same value are also effective. Another way to achieve contrast is to use warp and weft yarns of the same color, but one shiny and one dull. Strong color or value contrast between warp and weft tends to produce a busy overall effect.

Treadling as other weave structures. We have seen that we can borrow treadling keys from familiar block weaves and use them on a crackle threading with some interesting and useful results. I have tried treadling crackle as other block weaves such as Ms & Os. I have also tried treadling spot weaves such as huck and spot Bronson, in which treadling keys cannot be repeated to make tall blocks. Literal application of treadling keys for these structures to crackle was not as successful as I had hoped. The resulting fabrics tended to have an overall weft-emphasis with little pattern definition. I encourage you to try these treadlings for yourself. Then experiment to find other ways of treadling crackle that capture the spirit of the structure from which you borrowed treadlings.

Special Methods of Treadling

In addition to borrowing treadlings from other structures, we can use special treadling methods on crackle. These are just treadlings, in that they do not have threadings that "belong" to them to create a characteristic weave structure. Our weaving literature is replete with these treadling variations for use on overshot and summer & winter threadings. I can imagine those weavers sitting at their looms and doodling at the end of a warp, just to see what else could be done! Many of these references can be found in the Bibliography. Snyder (1961), Heather G. Thorpe (1956), Tod (1964), Zielinski (1981), and others suggest treadling variations specifically for use on crackle. I offer you a selection of my favorites.

Overshot variations. One variation on the idea of treadling pattern alternating with tabby was called *shadow weave* by Grace D. Blum (1960). This variation is not at all related to the weave structure we know as shadow weave. Simply switch the two wefts; what was the light tabby yarn now becomes pattern, and the former dark pattern yarn is used as tabby. Now the light pattern weft floats over a speckled light-dark background, giving a shadowy effect.

Another variation on the pattern-tabby alternation is called *shadow* by Snyder (1961). This variation is a way of making the pattern wefts appear less dense than in the ordinary overshot treadling, softening the strong crackle pattern blocks a bit. Alternate the pattern weft with two tabbies instead of one, for example, [2-a-b-2-a-b] instead of [2-a-2-b].

Lacy effects. In addition to the Bronson lace treadling, two other lace treadlings work particularly well on crackle. As in Bronson lace treadling, treadling keys for both are 6-pick repeats using a combination of pattern and tabby treadles. Both produce different lace blocks. Each of the lace treadling methods is quite distinct in appearance. It is worth sampling all three to determine which would work better in a particular project.

Mystery lace, as described by Marvin M. Morgenstern (1982), has a 5-pick repeat, similar to huck, e.g. [a-pattern-a-pattern-a]. Block treadling keys cannot be repeated. Any pattern tends to be obscured by overall weft dominance, and the cloth is not particularly lacy. Changing to a 6-pick sequence that includes both tabbies and just one pattern treadle in each block key, e.g. [a-pattern-a-b-pattern-b], allows us to make the blocks as tall as we would like and move from block to block at will. My block letter assignments are arbitrary; I selected the block with the strongest weft lace as the main pattern block, and derived the following treadling keys:

Block A:	a 2 a b 2 b
Block B:	a 3 a b 3 b
Block C:	a 4 a b 4 b
Block D:	a 1 a b 1 b

Another useful lace treadling for crackle was referred to as *two-block lace* by Blum (1960). The 6-pick treadling sequence involves alternating two adjacent pattern treadles twice, followed by *a* and *b*. Again, block letter assignments are arbitrary. Treadling keys are:

Block A:	1 2 1 2 a b
Block B:	2 3 2 3 a b
Block C:	3 4 3 4 a b
Block D:	4 1 4 1 a b

Complex block designs are difficult to see in these lace treadlings when warps and wefts match. But as the fabric moves in angled light, glimpses of the blocks flash. Mystery lace, shown in *Figure 3-18*, is quite textural and less open than the other two lace treadlings. Two-block lace (*Figure 3-19*) looks more smooth and elegant in the weft direction. Bronson lace treadling tends to be more open and lacy.

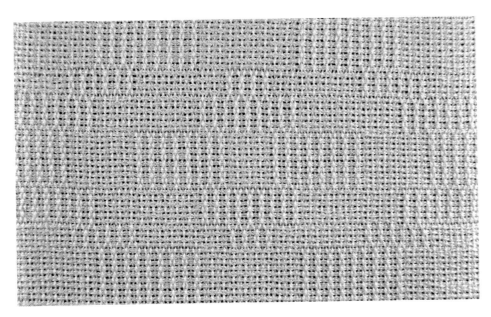

Figure 3-18. Sample woven as mystery lace.

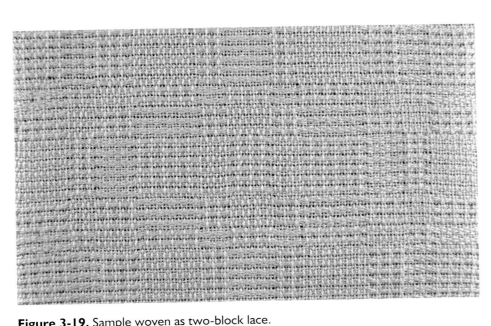

Figure 3-19. Sample woven as two-block lace.

One interesting way to use the lace treadlings is to make vertical stripes, rather than a complex motif with the blocks, by just repeating the treadling for one of the blocks. Combining lace stripes in the body of a table runner, for example, while treadling a border in a block motif using one of the other treadling methods is a trick I learned from Diantha States. Diantha has done extensive work combining lace with other treadling methods on overshot threadings in table linens and other household textiles. People often puzzle over how many shafts these items require. Just four! We looked at my linen table runner (*Figure 3-20*) inspired by Diantha and shown earlier in this chapter when I discussed the blue border woven in the manner of summer & winter. The solid white body of the runner is treadled as two-block lace. I determined which of the four block treadlings to use for the stripes by sampling all four. I then chose the one that seemed to carry the eye most pleasingly from the blue border into the white body of the runner.

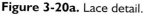

Figure 3-20a. Lace detail.

Figure 3-20b. Border detail.

Figure 3-20.
Table runner, linen and linen/rayon blend, woven as two-block lace with border woven as paired summer & winter.

On opposites. Weaving *on opposites* produces a weft-emphasis fabric with a pattern color dominant in two blocks and a background color dominant in the other two blocks. Tabby may be used but is not necessary. With an open sett, the completely weft-faced structure really shines for rugs. Frey (1975) recommends using tabby between pairs of opposites to improve the stability of weft-faced rugs. These tabbies will be buried by the pattern wefts.

Choose two contrasting colors for your wefts. Leading with the pattern color (black in *Figure 3-21*), place that first pick in one of the pattern sheds. Then follow with the background color (gray in *Figure 3-21*) in the opposite shed. The opposite is the shed made by lifting the shafts that weren't lifted for the first shed. For example, if you used Treadle 1, which lifts Shafts 3 and 4 for your main color, then use Treadle 3, which lifts Shafts 1 and 2, for your background color. There are four pairs of opposites, giving us four block treadling keys:

Block A:	2 4
Block B:	3 1
Block C:	4 2
Block D:	1 3

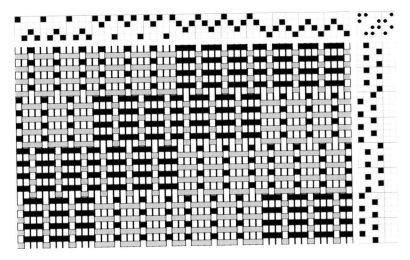

Figure 3-21. Treadled on opposites.

When crackle on opposites is not completely weft-faced, some warps show along the bottom of the blocks. Note the white warp floats along the bottoms of the black blocks in *Figure 3-21*. These bits of warp do show and can be quite distracting in the finished fabric, especially if the warp contrasts strongly in value with the weft colors. Compare the sample of our diamond motif woven on opposites in *Figure 3-22* with the weft-faced swatch in *Figure 3-23*, in which the warps are completely hidden.

Figure 3-22.
Sample woven
on opposites.

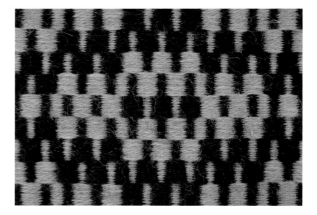

Figure 3-23.
Weft-faced sample
woven on opposites.

Swivel. For *swivel* treadling, and *honeycomb* which follows, we'll change our 2/2 twill tie-up to a 3/1 twill tie-up. With this unbalanced tie-up all the design action happens on the face of the cloth, with long floats on the back. These floats could limit the functionality of the cloth, but interesting effects on the face may be worth it. The 3/1 tie-up is:

4	4		4		4
3		3	3	3	
	2	2	2		2
1	1	1		1	
1	2	3	4	a	b

The chief characteristic of fabric treadled in the swivel manner is that patterns are composed of dots of color in plain weave, or nearly plain weave, on the face of the cloth. There are long floats on the back where wefts travel from one block to another. Imagine uses for these fabrics such as upholstery, pillows, bags, or other lined items where the floats on the back are protected and provide a bit of padding.

Swivel is constructed from "complementary" wefts, in which each is required in order to produce a structurally-sound fabric. Sometimes, "opposite" tabbies are used. Descriptions in the literature of how to weave swivel can be quite confusing. Complementary wefts are ones that "complete" a tabby combination. For instance, if the first weft goes into a shed with warps on Shaft 1 lifted, then its complement involves lifting warps on Shaft 3. But we use an unbalanced 3/1 tie-up for weaving swivel, lifting three shafts and leaving one down, in order to see the pattern rather than the long floats while we are weaving. We are concerned with the warp ends that remain down, or weren't lifted. Soon we are reading sentences that seem to have double negatives! I find it easiest to sit at the loom, with the reference in hand, and parse the sentences, stepping on treadles until I see how it works. Jean Scorgie's discussion of swivel (2011) greatly furthers understanding this unusual treadling method.

My favorite swivel treadling on crackle (*Figure 3-24*) has been called *petitpoint* by Helene Bress (1981), Morgenstern (1982), Margaret Windeknecht (1978), and others. Delicate pattern is composed of four blocks: one pattern block with dense dots of pattern color; one solid-color plain weave background block; and two intermediate half-tone blocks of dots in columns. On the back of the cloth (*Figure 3-24a*), pattern wefts float across the entire width of background blocks. Ground wefts float across the width of pattern blocks.

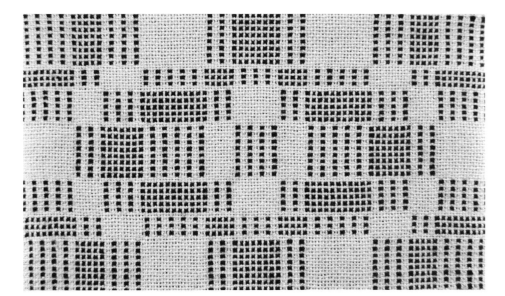

Figure 3-24. Sample woven as petitpoint swivel.

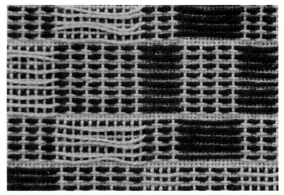

Figure 3-24a. Long floats on back.

The treadling sequence is one pattern shot in a contrasting pattern color, followed by two ground shots using yarn the same as the warp. The first ground is a complementary weft; the second ground is an opposite tabby. When the block is as tall as desired, you may need to insert an extra tabby to maintain the integrity of the plain weave background. Block treadling keys with extra or "incidental" tabbies shown in parentheses are:

Block A:	1 3 b (a)
Block B:	2 4 a (b)
Block C:	3 1 b (a)
Block D:	4 2 a (b)

Study the block treadling keys and the 3/1 tie-up in *Figure 3-25* to see if you can figure out complements and opposites.

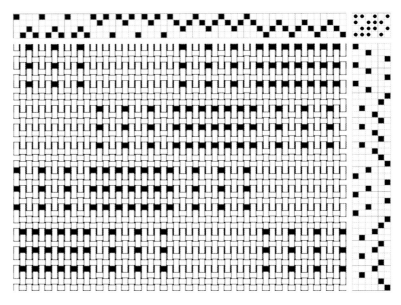

Figure 3-25. Treadled as petitpoint swivel.

Other swivel variations that are useful on crackle include *complementary weft tabby* (Barrett, 1979), *needlepoint swivel* (Blum, 1960), and *upholstery weave* (Bress, 1981). These all produce two blocks of pattern and two blocks of background. Weft picks may need to be added or deleted at the transition between blocks. Complementary weft tabby involves alternating pattern and background wefts on pairs of opposite pattern treadles, e.g. [1-3-2-4], [2-4-3-1], [3-1-4-2], and [4-2-1-3]. Needlepoint swivel alternates pattern and tabby, e.g. [1-b-2-a], [2-a-3-b], [3-b-4-a], and [4-a-1-b]. Upholstery weave uses two contrasting pattern weft colors. Two picks of the main color alternate with two picks of the background color. Treadling keys are straight twill: [1-2-3-4], [2-3-4-1], [3-4-1-2], and [4-1-2-3].

Honeycomb. Another group of treadlings that use the 3/1 tie-up are aptly named *honeycomb*. In these highly textural fabrics, oval-shaped cells are depressed and surrounded by raised outlines. The cells, usually woven in a contrasting color, are constructed by alternating two pattern shots until the cells are the desired height. Cell outlines, in a heavier weft the same color as the warp, are made by weaving one or two tabby shots between the cells. These heavy tabbies curve to fit around the cells. As expected, there are long pattern weft floats on the back of the cloth.

Crackle block motifs such as diamonds can be woven in honeycomb, although cell height is limited by warp floats the full height of the block on the front of the cloth, as seen in *Figure 3-26*. Block treadling keys for this sample are:

Block A:	a (heavy), then 1,2 (until desired height), then a (heavy)
Block B:	b (heavy), then 2,3 (until desired height), then b (heavy)
Block C:	a (heavy), then 3,4 (until desired height), then a (heavy)
Block D:	b (heavy), then 4,1 (until desired height), then b (heavy)

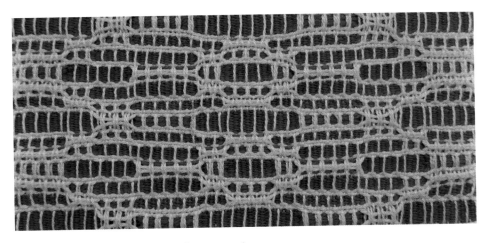

Figure 3-26. Sample woven as honeycomb.

Bress (1981) suggests that honeycomb treadlings work best on opposite blocks (or in the case of crackle, opposite *pairs* of blocks). She presents a comprehensive selection of honeycomb treadlings for overshot that would be well worth trying on crackle. Some variations include using two tabby outlines between cells, varying heights of cells, alternating colors in cells, weaving all one color, and stacking single block repeats to create vertical stripes.

Experiment on your crackle sampler with treadling methods in this chapter and many more that can be found in the literature. Then invent your own. My workshop students frequently come up with interesting treadlings when they make "mistakes" in a particular sample. I encourage you to document your variations, as you might want to weave them again.

Chapter **4**
Weave It Polychrome

Polychrome is a term that produces gorgeous fabrics and spirited discussion about its definition among weavers. Webster's dictionary defines polychrome as "being of many or various colors." Just because a textile has many colors, is it polychrome? And how many colors qualify as "many or various?" A review of the literature has led me to the following working definition.

First, polychrome, in the context of weaving, refers to a way of weaving that puts various colors side by side in the cloth. Because it's a treadling method, polychrome is created by wefts, not warps, so warp stripes alone (as in the scarf in Chapter 3 *Figure 3-10*) would not be polychrome. Second, although we can put multiple colors side-by-side with discontinuous wefts, as in tapestry, this also is not polychrome as the term is used in the literature. The term polychrome refers to a treadling method in which wefts of different colors are woven one after the other, selvedge-to-selvedge, and yet the colors *appear* to be side-by-side. The polychrome effect is created by weave structure, not by the weaver's manipulation of weft placement. And finally, how many colors make it polychrome? Two or more, or more than two? I'll leave that for you to decide.

There are a number of treadling methods in the block weave literature that either are specifically called polychrome, or make different colors appear next to each other in the woven cloth. These treadling methods are such valuable tools for use on crackle that I decided to devote an entire chapter to polychrome techniques for 4-shaft crackle. For all of these treadlings we will continue to use the standard 2/2 twill tie-up shown in Chapter 2. We'll look at polychrome crackle created with two, three, and four wefts. There is one method that I have found especially exciting with crackle. We'll take an extensive look at how to design with that method in the last part of the chapter.

Two Wefts

On opposites. We learned how to weave crackle on opposites in Chapter 3. Two weft colors alternate in opposite sheds, making wide and narrow columns of the two colors side by side. The cloth can be weft-faced, or the warp can show.

To illustrate several of the polychrome crackle techniques, I designed a series of towels. A navy blue warp of 8/2 unmercerized cotton was sett for plain weave at 18 e.p.i.. Four colors, magenta, peach, blue, and turquoise, were available to use for wefts. Crackle blocks were threaded in point order, A-B-C-D-C-B, and treadled straight, A-B-C-D, making zigzags. *Figure 4-1* shows the towel woven on opposites, with tabby. Pattern weft colors are blue and magenta; tabby matches warp.

Figure 4-1.
Towel fabric, woven on opposites.

Broken twill polychrome. Nancy Lyon (1987) discusses several polychrome methods, commenting that crackle "lets me blend many weft colors within and across threaded blocks, creating the illusion of complex threading on four harnesses." One method is a broken twill treadling order with two colors, although she notes more colors could be used. Block treadling keys are: [1-2-4-3], [2-3-1-4], [3-4-2-1], and [4-1-3-2].

Polychrome blocks. Snyder (1961) gives us a treadling for crackle that she calls *polychrome blocks*. Work with four weft colors, but only two at a time. Weave in the overshot manner, pattern alternating with tabby until you are ready to change blocks. Drop the pattern color, move the tabby color into the pattern position, and add a third color as tabby. Continue this color rotation through all four blocks and four colors. *Figures 4-2* and *4-3* show the navy blue towel warp woven in polychrome blocks in two different color sequences.

Below left:
Figure 4-2.
Towel fabric, woven as Snyder's polychrome blocks.

Below right:
Figure 4-3.
A different color order in Snyder's polychrome blocks.

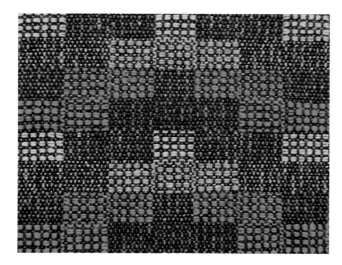

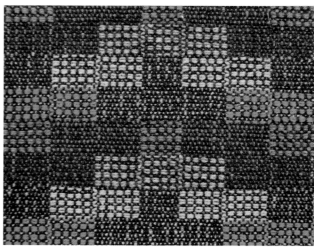

Three Wefts

Weaving in the Italian manner. In the weaving literature, *Italian manner* or *Italian style* refers to polychrome treadling with three colors. Lyon's (1987) Italian style crackle weaves 3-pick straight twill repeats: [1-2-3], [2-3-4], [3-4-1], and [4-1-2]. Repeat each sequence until the block is the desired height; then move to the next sequence. The three-weft color order remains the same throughout. No tabby is used. In *Figure 4-4* weft colors are peach, blue, and turquoise. Two pattern blocks show equal amounts of two different pairs of weft colors, turquoise and blue or turquoise and peach. Two background blocks each have dominant floats of one of the colors, peach or blue. The surface of the cloth is smooth.

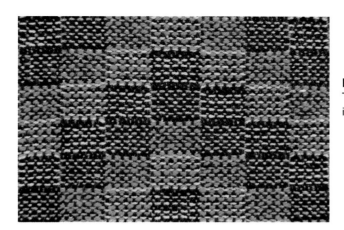

Figure 4-4.
Towel fabric, woven
in the Italian manner.

Classic crackle. Classic crackle, the subject of Chapter 2, is in fact a polychrome treadling with three wefts and is one of the Italian manner treadlings. Two ground wefts alternate with a pattern weft and with each other, in a 3-pick point twill order. Although the same pattern weft dominates in the two pattern blocks, they look different from each other due to the interaction of different ground weft colors with pattern color. The two background blocks are also different from each other, one showing mostly one ground weft color *(x)*, the other mostly the other ground color *(y)*. In the towel in *Figure 4-5*, pattern weft is magenta and ground wefts are blue and green. Unfortunately, in this sample the blue and green grounds are close in both hue and value and difficult to distinguish from each other. The surface of the cloth is more textural than Lyon's Italian style, because pattern wefts are paired together in columns in the pattern blocks.

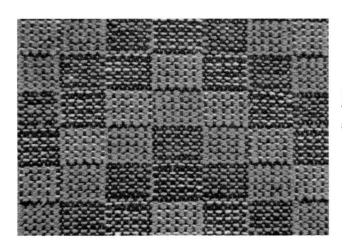

Figure 4-5.
Towel fabric, woven
as classic crackle.

Atwater (1928), Thorpe (1956), Snyder (1961), and Tod (1964) all present treadlings for crackle that they call *Italian manner*. One pattern color and two ground colors are used. On closer examination, we can see that these treadlings are the same as classic crackle within the blocks, but the sequences start and end with pattern rather than ground. For example, the Block A treadling key is [2 pattern-3 ground x-2 pattern-1 ground y- incidental on 2 (pattern) to end the block]. In classic crackle Block A is [1 ground x-2 pattern-3 ground y-2 pattern- incidental on 1 (ground x) to end the block].

Traditional polychrome crackle. The treadling that is traditionally referred to as *polychrome* in the overshot and crackle literature involves using two pattern wefts in two different colors on adjacent treadles alternating with tabby. As an overshot treadling variation, Bress (1981) and Morgenstern (1983) call this treadling *echo*. On crackle, the two pattern wefts show equally in one pattern block and one background block has dots of pattern colors. There are two intermediate blocks, one with floats of one pattern color, the other with floats of the other pattern color. In the towel fabric shown in *Figure 4-6*, pattern colors are magenta and turquoise. Tabby is navy blue, same as warp. This method has become my favorite polychrome treadling for crackle. Later in this chapter we'll learn much more about drafting and designing traditional polychrome crackle.

Figure 4-6. Towel fabric, woven as traditional polychrome crackle.

Four Wefts

Flamepoint boundweave. Perhaps a better name for boundweave is *weft-faced pattern weaves*, as noted by Nancy Arthur Hoskins (1992) in her book by that same name. A broad category of treadling methods, boundweave encompasses a number of the polychrome treadlings when woven weft-faced. *Figure 4-7* shows weft-faced on opposites. *Figure 4-8* is weft-faced Italian manner and *4-9* is classic crackle. Rug weavers will delight in these weft-faced polychrome options for crackle.

Figure 4-7.
Weft-faced sample woven on opposites.

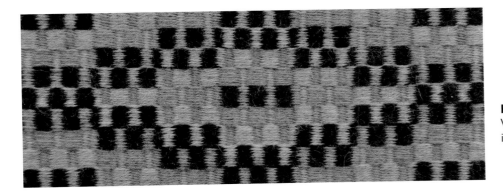

Figure 4-8.
Weft-faced sample woven in the Italian manner.

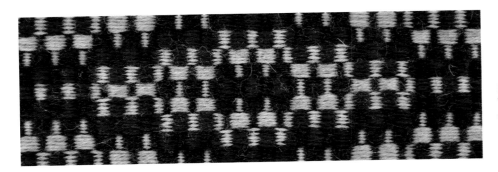

Figure 4-9.
Weft-faced sample woven as classic crackle.

One common boundweave treadling with four colors is often called *flamepoint* boundweave, shown in *Figure 4-10*. On crackle, Lyon(1987) calls it *shaded twill*; Snyder (1961) calls it *no tabby weave*. Flamepoint boundweave is a color-rotation weave, in which the block treadling keys are created by a rotation of colors, not a change in treadling. Treadling is for straight twill, [1-2-3-4], with four shuttles. Select four weft colors and arrange the four shuttles in your starting color order. When the block is as tall as desired, rotate the first color to the back of the order, and resume treadling [1-2-3-4]. Continue through all four color rotations to get the four crackle blocks. Reverse color rotations when your block order changes from ascending to descending.

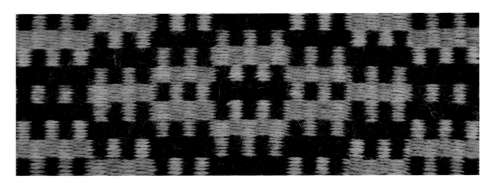

Figure 4-10.
Weft-faced sample woven
as flamepoint boundweave.

On crackle, different pairs of the four colors show in each block. You may have to do a bit of sampling to decide the best color order to start with to show your design motif. One way is to start by arranging your weft colors by value, darkest to lightest. Frequently I sit at the loom and step on treadles until I see which two treadles will put "pattern" in the first block called for in my motif. I put the two dominant or darkest colors in those two sheds and arrange the other colors accordingly. That gives me my starting color order.

Flamepoint boundweave does not have to be woven weft-faced. This treadling produces an entirely twill structure on crackle. In a balanced fabric the warp shows and is part of the design; the cloth is smooth and drapeable. Stunning color blending can be achieved in fine fabrics suitable for wearables. *Figure 4-11* shows the towel fabric with all four pattern weft colors: magenta, peach, blue, and turquoise.

Figure 4-11.
Towel fabric,
woven as
flamepoint
boundweave.

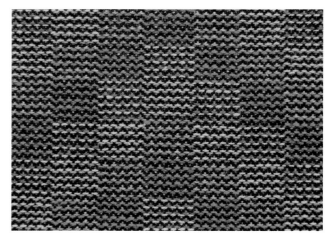

Designing Traditional Polychrome Crackle

Characteristics. Traditional polychrome crackle has captured my attention for its ability to produce four distinctly different blocks with two pattern wefts and a tabby. Compare the two towel fabrics in *Figures 4-12* and *4-13*. We first saw this Atwater design in Chapter 3 *Figure 3-8* treadled in the overshot manner. That towel is shown again *Figure 4-12* in a detail of the block layout. Warp and tabby are white. Pattern weft is blue and turquoise wound together on one bobbin. *Figure 4-13* shows the same towel treadled traditional polychrome, with light red and orange pattern wefts, each on its own shuttle. How exciting!

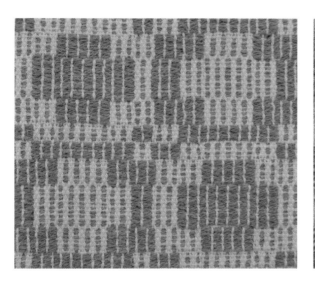

Figure 4-12.
Towel fabric, woven in the overshot manner.

Figure 4-13.
Towel fabric, woven as traditional polychrome crackle.

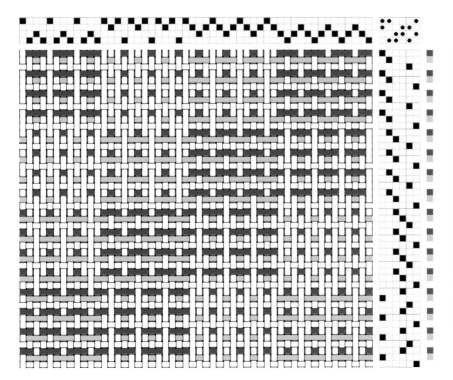

Figure 4-14. Treadled as traditional polychrome crackle.

No longer do we have two pattern blocks and two background blocks in our crackle designs. Instead, there is one pattern block showing equal amounts of the two pattern colors stacked up in alternating columns. One background block shows mostly the ground color created primarily by warp and tabby interlacement. Tabby can match the warp color or be different. Dots of both pattern colors show in the background block. The other two blocks are intermediate. One block has floats of one pattern color; the other floats of the other pattern color. Identify these four types of blocks in the structural draft in *Figure 4-14*.

Our familiar diamond motif from Chapter 3 is shown in traditional polychrome crackle in *Figure 4-15*. Pattern wefts are dark blue and turquoise. Warp and tabby are natural cotton.

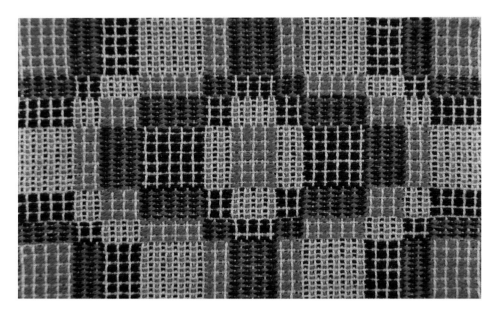

Figure 4-15. Sample woven as traditional polychrome crackle.

Treadling. The treadling sequence is a rhythmic 6-pick sequence: [**pattern color x-pattern color y in the next pattern shed-tabby-pattern x-pattern y-other tabby**]. Block treadling keys for traditional polychrome crackle are:

Block A:	1 2 a 1 2 b
Block B:	2 3 a 2 3 b
Block C:	3 4 a 3 4 b
Block D:	4 1 a 4 1 b

In *Figure 4-15* note the diamond motif created by the nearly weft-faced blue and turquoise pattern blocks. Background blocks are the opposite blocks, those not adjacent to the pattern blocks in the A-B-C-D order. In this sample, the turquoise intermediate blocks show around the outside of the diamond and the dark blue intermediates show on the inside. The location of colors of intermediate blocks can be reversed by reversing the pattern weft order in the treadling sequence. For instance, if the color order in *Figure 4-15* is turquoise-blue-tabby, change to blue-turquoise-tabby to put the dark blue around the outside of the diamond and turquoise inside.

Sometimes, changing the order of pattern weft colors can make a dramatic difference not only in a single motif but also in the overall pattern of a fabric with repeated motifs. Compare the towels in *Figures 4-16* and *4-17*. One towel leads with red, followed by orange; the other towel leads with orange, followed by red. It's hard to believe they are identical except for the order of pattern wefts in treadling.

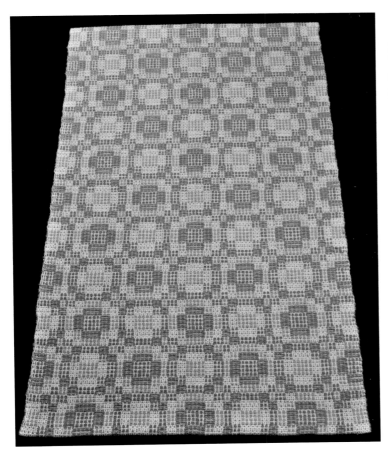

Figure 4-16.
Towel woven
as traditional
polychrome crackle.

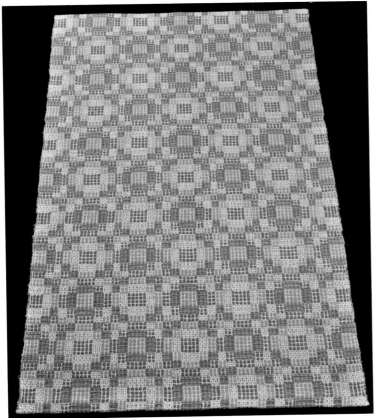

Figure 4-17.
Towel, traditional
polychrome crackle,
color order reversed.

Figure 4-18a. Detail.

Design decisions. As we have seen, color order is one important design decision. In repeating patterns with small blocks, as in the red-orange towels on page 59, it is generally better to choose one color order and stay with it throughout the piece. Otherwise, the design can get confusing. An exception is if you plan a border at each end of the piece, as for a table runner or the ends of a scarf. Sometimes changing the color order can make the border distinct from the body yet still coordinated with it.

With large blocks in a less busy pattern, as in the wool throw in *Figure 4-18,* there is opportunity not only to change color order from block to block, but also to change to different pattern colors when blocks change. Four pattern weft colors are used in the throw. Once I had designed my block order in threading and treadling, I decided which two colors to use in any given block. I then determined the color order to use in treadling based on which color I wanted in which intermediate block.

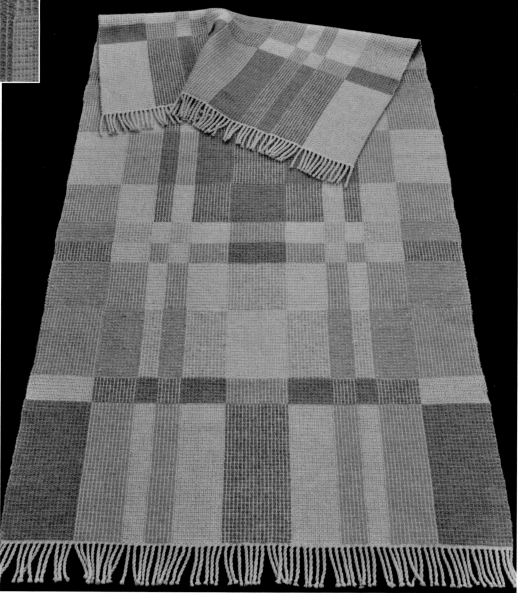

Figure 4-18.
Throw, wool, woven as
traditional polychrome
crackle.

Value can be at least as important as, if not more important than, hue in the design. *Figures 4-19* and *4-20* show two table runners woven on the same natural linen warp. Block arrangement is *exactly the same* in both runners. Each has four pattern weft colors, used two at a time. I chose a different pair of pattern wefts each time I changed to treadling a new block. The colors for the runner in *Figure 4-19* are brown, coral, dark red, and gray blue-green. For *4-20*, colors are gray blue-green, medium yellow green, taupe, and celadon. Note how different the two runners look.

Figure 4-19a. Detail.

Figure 4-19.
Traditional polychrome crackle table runner, linen and linen/cotton/ rayon blend.

Figure 4-20a.
Detail.

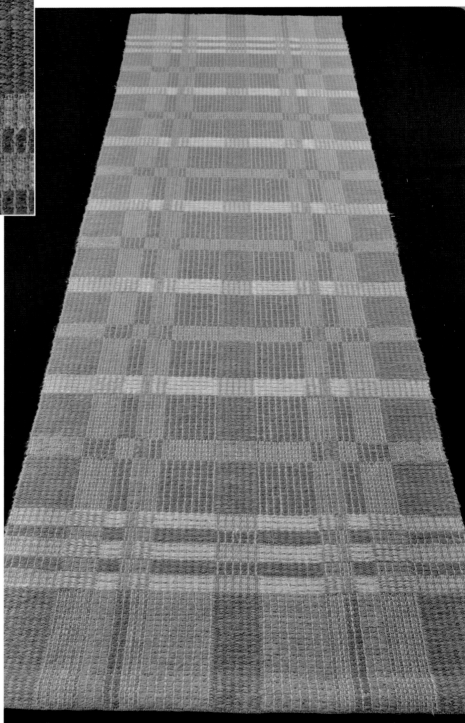

Figure 4-20.
Traditional polychrome
crackle table runner, linen and
linen/cotton/rayon blend.

Design process. Although my computer weave drafting programs are essential time-savers in most of my design work, I have found that the quickest and easiest way to design traditional 4-shaft polychrome crackle is with old-fashioned graph paper and colored pencils. I then might go to the computer for fine-tuning, and invariably make some changes at the loom. Finally, when the project is off the loom and finished, there is occasionally a surprise. The transparent effect in the center blocks of the throw (*Figure 4-18*) was unplanned but welcome.

Start designing traditional polychrome crackle by choosing two pattern weft colors. For the following illustrations, blue and red are the pattern colors. We'll assume the warp and tabby are white. Draw a profile threading on your graph paper. Under the profile threading outline the pattern blocks in the order and heights you wish to weave them. Fill in these pattern blocks with both colors equally. In *Figure 4-21*, I have designed my block layout and filled in the pattern blocks with purple, which is a blend of my two pattern colors, red and blue. The opposite (non-adjacent) blocks to the pattern blocks will be background blocks. Leave those blocks white.

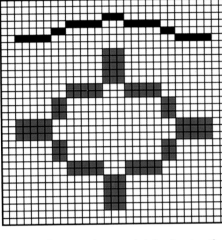

Figure 4-21. Pattern blocks (where pattern weft colors blend) are entered.

Next, fill in one of the adjacent blocks with one of the pattern weft colors, shown as blue in *Figure 4-22*. Then, color the other adjacent blocks with the second pattern weft color, red (*Figure 4-23*). Look at the first row of blocks in the design. You will see that Block D is the pattern block (purple). Block B, the opposite block to D, is background (white). One adjacent block, Block A, is blue; Block C, the other adjacent block, is red.

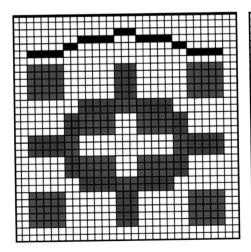

Figure 4-22. Pattern weft color entered in one adjacent block.

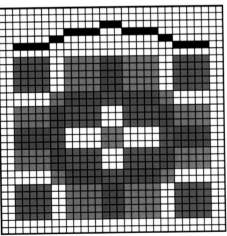

Figure 4-23. Pattern weft colors entered in both adjacent blocks.

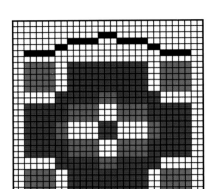

Figure 4-24. Pattern colors reversed in order from *4-23*.

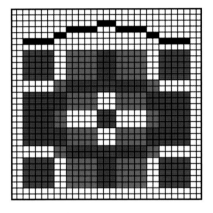

Figure 4-25. Color order changes with each block treadling change.

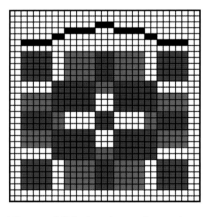

Figure 4-26. Another color order.

Try sketching the same block design, but with the colors in adjacent blocks reversed (*Figure 4-24*). You may like this arrangement better. Then try changing the adjacent color positions again. You can change the color order with each change in block treadling. In *Figure 4-25*, at times blue is in the block that precedes the pattern block and other times it is in the following block. *Figure 4-26* shows yet another possibility. Note that the purple pattern blocks have remained in the same position in all of these profile cloth diagrams.

Once you have decided on your block layout, you'll need to figure out the order in which to weave the two pattern wefts for each block. Remember our block treadling keys:

Block A:	1 (color x), 2 (color y), a, 1 (color x), 2 (color y), b
Block B:	2 (color x), 3 (color y), a, 2 (color x), 3 (color y), b
Block C:	3 (color x), 4 (color y), a, 3 (color x), 4 (color y), b
Block D:	4 (color x), 1 (color y), a, 4 (color x), 1 (color y), b

For each block in your treadling order you will need to determine which color is x and which is y. One way is to step on treadles at your loom until you see which color to weave first. Or, you can follow your cloth diagram block by block and use the following chart to assign colors:

Pattern Block A:	color x is in Block D, color y is in Block B
Pattern Block B:	color x is in Block A, color y is in Block C
Pattern Block C:	color x is in Block B, color y is in Block D
Pattern Block D:	color x is in Block C, color y is in Block A

Let's use *Figure 4-26* as an example. The first block that is treadled to make the design has pattern (purple) in Block D. The chart above tells us that if pattern is in D, then color x will be in Block C. Look at our design and you will see that Block C is red; therefore, color x is red and color y is blue. The next block calls for pattern in Block C. Block B is blue in the cloth diagram; therefore, it is color x and red is color y.

Crackle's blocks are not independent of each other, which is a distinct advantage with polychrome treadlings. Colors can blend together in some blocks or appear alone in others. Traditional polychrome crackle in particular is an exciting way to get the look of complex designs with many colors on just four shafts. In Chapter 5, we'll see what happens when we weave crackle on more than four shafts.

Chapter 5
More Shafts – More Blocks

Crackle on more shafts retains the characteristics of 4-shaft crackle. The number of blocks possible equals the number of shafts available. We can have six blocks with six shafts, eight blocks with eight shafts, and so on. More blocks mean more potential design complexity. As in 4-shaft crackle, blocks are not independent of each other. There are no floats longer than three ends or picks.

As you can see in the 8-shaft crackle design in *Figure 5-1*, our familiar pattern blocks and background blocks appear, plus a third structural element. That third element is plain weave, or nearly plain weave, depending on the treadling method. It acts as a smooth half-tone background on which the pattern blocks and background blocks seem to float. In order to distinguish the three types of blocks in multi-shaft crackle, I choose to call the blocks in this third structural element "background" blocks. I will refer to the blocks that were formerly called background blocks in 4-shaft crackle as "reverse-pattern" blocks, because they are structurally the same as the reverse side of the pattern blocks.

Because its blocks are cleaner and easier to see, I'll use crackle woven in the overshot manner for the drafting discussion. Later in the chapter we'll explore multi-shaft classic crackle and several other treadling variations.

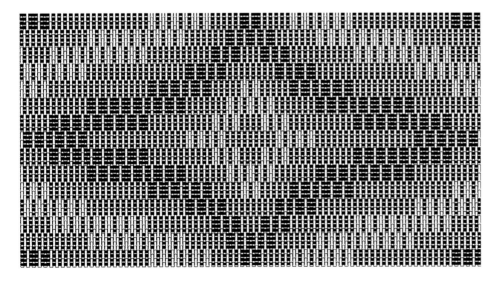

Figure 5-1.
An 8-shaft crackle design.

Threading and Treadling More Blocks

Threading keys. To derive crackle threading keys for more shafts, simply extend the same 3-shaft point twill threadings over as many shafts as you plan to use. For the last two blocks, remember to wrap your threading around to Shafts 1 and 2 in order to get all possible blocks. Threading keys for eight crackle blocks on eight shafts are:

Block A:	1 2 3 2 (1)
Block B:	2 3 4 3 (2)
Block C:	3 4 5 4 (3)
Block D:	4 5 6 5 (4)
Block E:	5 6 7 6 (5)
Block F:	6 7 8 7 (6)
Block G:	7 8 1 8 (7)
Block H:	8 1 2 1 (8)

Incidentals. Thread incidentals on the same shaft that started the block to complete the block. These incidentals are shown in parentheses in the threading keys above. As we discussed in Chapter 2, use of these incidentals as "the period at the end of the sentence" is not optional. Otherwise, changes in float length can occur.

If you wish to skip blocks in your threading, incidentals get a little more complicated. The goal is to maintain the odd-even threading order. You have two choices for how to handle incidentals. The first possibility is to add one extra incidental for each skipped block. For example, to move directly from Block B, which ends on Shaft 2, to Block F, which starts on Shaft 6, thread the incidentals for Blocks C through E (Shafts 3, 4, and 5) in between. *Figure 5-2* shows this incidental method. Note the slight separation of Blocks B and F at the corners where they meet.

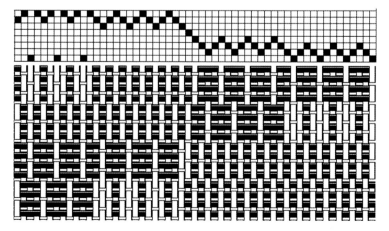

Figure 5-2. Use one incidental for each skipped block.

The other option for incidentals between skipped blocks is to use one incidental or none, whichever is needed to preserve the odd-even threading sequence. In our example above, skipping from Block B ending on Shaft 2 and Block F starting on Shaft 6, an extra incidental is needed. *Figure 5-3* shows the extra incidental on Shaft 3. With this method, Blocks B and F touch at the corners. Differences are slight between the two methods, but they warrant comparison to get the effect you want in your design. Remember that if you return to the beginning of the draft and thread Block B after F, you will again need to decide how to handle incidentals for the skipped blocks. In designs with reflection symmetry, use the same incidental method on both sides of a motif.

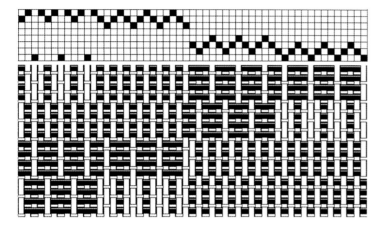

Figure 5-3. Use one extra incidental to preserve odd-even threading sequence.

In the pillow shown in *Figure 5-4*, I wanted to make a "clean break" between motifs, but didn't use either of these options for handling incidentals between skipped blocks. In going from Block D to Block H, I used no transitional incidentals. This break in the odd-even sequence is obvious. In the detail photo, you can see lines of light tabby weft floating over two warps between motifs, which tends to detract from the overall design.

Figure 5-4.
8-shaft crackle pillow, wool, cotton, and linen/cotton/rayon blend, woven as overshot.

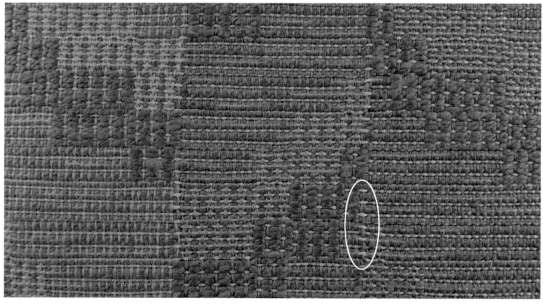

Figure 5-4a.
Detail. Notice the tabby floating over two warps.

Treadling keys. Treadling multi-shaft crackle as overshot is the same as for 4-shaft crackle. Pattern alternates with tabby. Block treadling keys for 8-shaft crackle, using the tie-ups that follow, are:

Block A:	1 a 1 b
Block B:	2 a 2 b
Block C:	3 a 3 b
Block D:	4 a 4 b
Block E:	5 a 5 b
Block F:	6 a 6 b
Block G:	7 a 7 b
Block H:	8 a 8 b

So how do we get the three design areas, pattern, reverse-pattern, and background? The secret is in the tie-up.

It's All in the Tie-Up

Twill ratios. The twill tie-up ratio is a powerful design tool for working with any twill-based weave. Ratios are expressed with numbers above and below a line. For a rising shed tie-up, numbers above the line refer to shafts that are raised; those below the line are shafts that remain down. In the 2/2 ratio that we used for 4-shaft crackle, each pattern treadle has two adjacent shafts tied up and the next pair of adjacent shafts stay down. Pattern blocks are created by pattern wefts floating over warps that remain down. Background blocks are created by raised warps floating over pattern wefts.

To preserve crackle's characteristics, its multi-shaft tie-up ratios must have at least one number *2* below the line to create pairs of pattern blocks and one number *2* above the line to create a pair of reverse-pattern blocks. For 6- or 8-shaft crackle, the remaining numbers in the ratio are *1*, alternately above and below the line, which ties up plain weave. This part of the ratio creates that third design area, the background blocks. The total of all numbers above and below the line equals the number of shafts being used. As shorthand, I'll use the notation 2/2/1/1 to express the 6-shaft ratio $\frac{2\ \ 1}{2\ \ 1}$.

To derive a tie-up from a ratio, make the first pattern treadle in your tie-up by tying up or leaving untied each shaft according to the numbers in the ratio. Enter the shafts into the tie-up grid reading from bottom to top. The first treadle in the 6-shaft ratio 2/2/1/1 would tie up Shafts 1 and 2, leave Shafts 3 and 4 untied, tie up Shaft 5, and leave Shaft 6 untied. Once you have the first treadle entered in the tie-up grid, you can determine each succeeding treadle by tying it in the same order, but starting the ratio by stepping up one square to make the twill diagonal. Here is a 6-shaft tie-up for crackle with a ratio of 2/2/1/1:

	1	2	3	4	5	6	a	b
6		6			6	6		6
5	5			5	5		5	
4			4	4		4		4
3		3	3		3		3	
2	2	2		2				2
1	1		1			1	1	
	1	2	3	4	5	6	a	b

Looking at Treadle 1 and reading from the bottom, you can see that first there are two shafts up, then two down, one up, and one down. This corresponds to the numbers in the ratio. Once you have derived a tie-up, re-order the pattern treadles if needed so that Treadle 1 produces pattern in Blocks A and B. Tabby *a* ties odd shafts 1-3-5 and tabby *b* ties even shafts 2-4-6.

Figure 5-5 shows what 6-shaft crackle looks like when we use this 2/2/1/1 tie-up. Blocks are threaded and treadled in straight A-B-C-D-E-F order. There are two pattern blocks, two reverse-pattern blocks, and two background blocks. As would be expected from the tie-up, reverse-pattern blocks (the two shafts up) precede pattern blocks (the two shafts down) across the alphabetical block order.

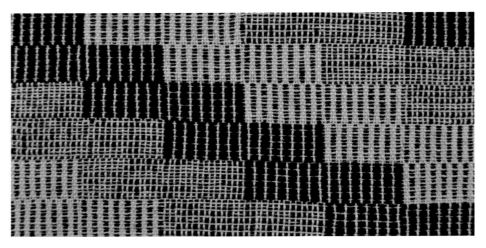

Figure 5-5. 6-shaft crackle sample, 2/2/1/1 tie-up.

Another option for a 6-shaft tie-up would be to put the reverse-pattern blocks *after* the pattern blocks in the design. Change the ratio so that the first *2* is below the line, followed by a *2* above the line. Ratios typically start with a number above the line, so this ratio would be written 1/2/2/1 and is illustrated in *Figure 5-6*.

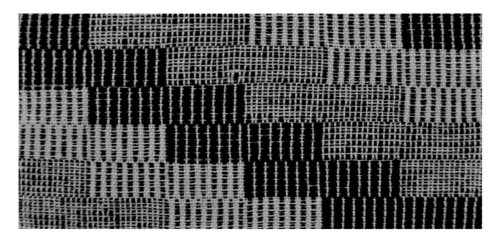

Figure 5-6. 6-shaft crackle sample, 1/2/2/1 tie-up.

Now let's think about ratios for 8-shaft crackle. With eight blocks, we can have two pattern blocks, two reverse-pattern blocks, and four background blocks. Snyder's *The Crackle Weave* (1961) was the earliest reference I found for crackle on more than four shafts. Snyder gave just one tie-up for eight shafts, with the ratio 2/2/1/1/1/1. Reverse-pattern blocks precede pattern with this tie-up. In my work for the COE in 1990 and my samples for Strickler (1991), this was the only tie-up I knew and used for 8-shaft crackle. *Figures 5-7* and *5-8* show two examples of my designs that were not included in Carol Strickler's book.

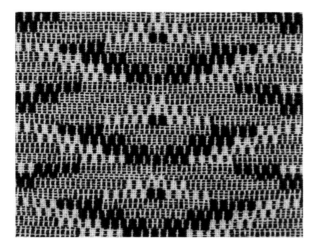

Figure 5-7.

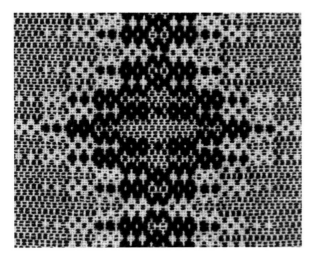

Figure 5-8.

As I experimented more with multi-shaft crackle, it occurred to me that I could change the position of the reverse-pattern blocks relative to pattern blocks. They could even be completely separated from each other by pairs of background blocks. And this manipulation could be accomplished in the tie-up. *Figures 5-9, 5-11*, and *5-13* show these three tie-ups, labeled *a*, *b*, and *c*. Next to the tie-ups are the corresponding woven samples (*Figures 5-10, 5-12,* and *5-14*) that I included in my 1995 article in *Weaver's* magazine. Some time after publishing that article, I found Wanda Shelp's and Carol Wostenberg's excellent 1991 book, *Eight Shafts: A Place to Begin*, that contains these

1	2	3	4	5	6	7	8	a	b
8		8		8			8		8
	7		7			7	7	7	
6		6			6	6			6
	5			5	5		5	5	
4			4	4		4			4
	3	3		3			3	3	
	2	2		2		2			2
1	1		1		1				1

Figure 5-9. Tie-up *a*, 2/2/1/1/1/1 ratio.

1	2	3	4	5	6	7	8	a	b
	8		8	8			8		8
7		7	7			7		7	
	6	6			6		6		6
5	5			5		5		5	
4			4		4		4		4
	3		3			3	3	3	
	2		2		2	2			2
1		1		1	1				1

Figure 5-11. Tie-up *b*, 1/2/2/1/1/1 ratio.

1	2	3	4	5	6	7	8	a	b
	8	8		8			8		8
7	7		7			7		7	
6		6			6		6	6	6
	5			5		5	5	5	
4			4	4	4				4
	3		3	3			3	3	
	2		2	2		2			2
1		1	1		1				1

Figure 5-13. Tie-up *c*, 2/1/1/2/1/1 ratio.

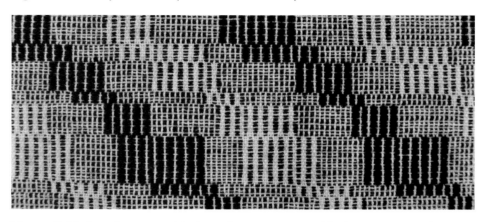

Figure 5-10. Sample, reverse-pattern blocks precede pattern blocks.

Figure 5-12. Sample, reverse-pattern blocks follow pattern blocks.

Figure 5-14. Sample, pattern blocks and reverse-pattern blocks are separated.

same three tie-ups, along with a wealth of crackle information and patterns. Pattern treadles in the three tie-ups have been re-ordered so that Treadle 1 produces pattern in Blocks A and B, Treadle 2 makes pattern in B and C, Treadle 3 pattern in C and D, and so on through the twill order. Tabby *a* is tied to odd-numbered shafts, 1-3-5-7, and tabby *b* to even shafts, 2-4-6-8.

Other tie-up possibilities. Are there other tie-ups that could be used for 8-shaft crackle, and still produce true crackle? Let's examine a few possibilities.

Using a 2/2/2/2 tie-up, which eliminates the plain weave 1/1/1/1 part of the ratio, results in cloth that is exactly like 4-shaft crackle (*Figure 5-15*).

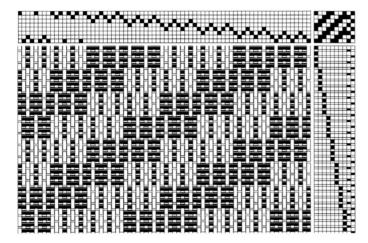

Figure 5-15. 2/2/2/2 tie-up.

Any numbers other than *1* or *2* in the ratio change the float length, and we no longer have true crackle. *Figure 5-16* shows just how long the floats are when we use a 3/3/1/1 tie-up. Pattern wefts float over eleven ends on both the front and back. Depending on yarns and ultimate use of the fabric, floats this long may not be practical.

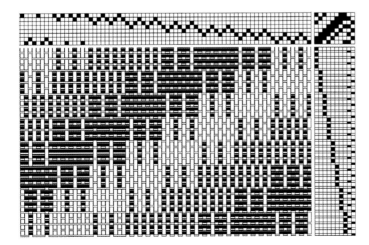

Figure 5-16. 3/3/1/1 tie-up.

If we combine the numbers *1, 2*, and *3* in the ratio, as in *3/2/1/2*, we get fabric that looks different on the front and back. *Figure 5-17* shows the front, *Figure 5-18* is a back view. Again, because of the 11-end float on the back, this is not true crackle, but may be useful. In addition to pattern, reverse-pattern, and background areas, we now get a fourth design element. There is solid color true plain weave constructed by warp and tabby weft on the front in those blocks that have the long pattern weft floats on the back.

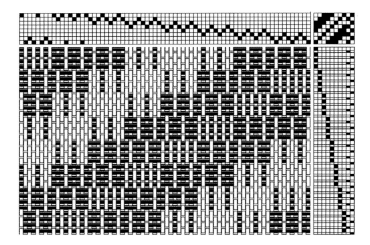

Figure 5-17. 3/2/1/2 tie-up, front.

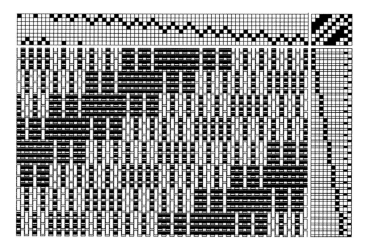

Figure 5-18. 3/2/1/2 tie-up, back.

Until now, we have considered only balanced tie-up ratios, in which the total of the numbers above the line equals the total below the line. Ralph Griswold (2004) suggests two unbalanced tie-ups that produce fabric that is very different on the front and back, but is true crackle because float length does not exceed three ends. *Figures 5-19* and *5-20* illustrate front and back of crackle using the tie-up ratio 1/1/2/1/2/1. The two sides are distinctly different. There are two pairs of reverse-pattern blocks and no pattern blocks on the front. On the back are two pairs of pattern blocks and no reverse-pattern blocks. Griswold's second ratio, 1/1/1/2/1/2, produces the opposite effect from *Figures 5-19* and *5-20*, pattern on front and reverse-pattern on back. Griswold's tie-ups could be very useful when you are designing fabric that will be viewed from both sides, such as a scarf. You also could combine fabric pieces with front and back sides out in a garment, getting the effect of two different but coordinated fabrics from only one length of yardage.

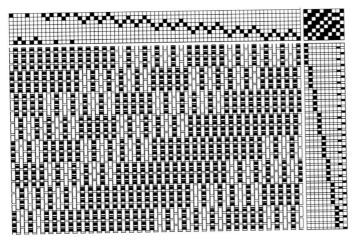

Figure 5-19. Griswold's 1/1/2/1/2/1 tie-up, front.

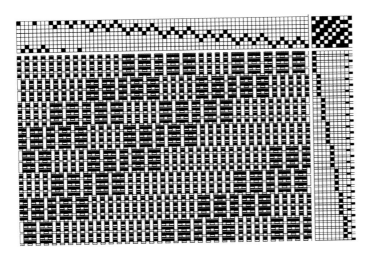

Figure 5-20. Griswold's 1/1/2/1/2/1 tie-up, back.

Crackle on odd numbers of shafts. I used to believe that crackle could be only woven on an even numbers of shafts. We frequently see 4-, 6- and 8-shaft crackle in our literature. Then I spotted Mary Elizabeth Laughlin's (1976) mention of 7-shaft crackle. Her tie-up ratio is 2/2/1/2. Because the totals of numbers above and below the ratio line are different, we would expect the cloth to look different on front and back. *Figures 5-21* and *5-22* illustrate front and back of Laughlin's tie-up for seven blocks of crackle.

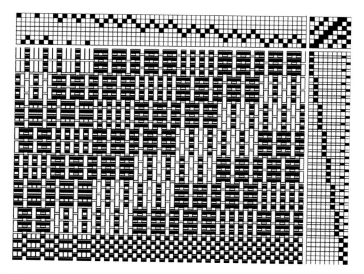

Figure 5-21. 7-shaft crackle, Laughlin's 2/2/1/2 tie-up, front.

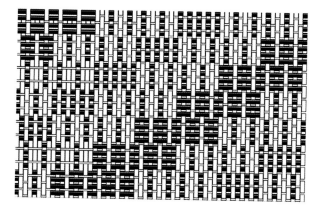

Figure 5-22. Laughlin's 2/2/1/2 tie-up, back.

Look closely at the draft in *Figure 5-21* to see how block structures change with seven shafts. First, true plain weave cannot be woven across all blocks. Tabby treadles are tied to 1-3-5-7 and 2-4-6. I have added a bit of plain weave treadling at the bottom of the draft. You can see that we get plain weave in Blocks A through E, but not in Blocks F and G. On both sides of the cloth, in the first five blocks there are two pattern blocks, two reverse-pattern, and one background. The last two blocks, F and G, are structurally not crackle. Float length does remain at a maximum of three in those two blocks, but "tabby" also has long floats. These blocks might have an interesting texture where warps are bundled together by longer floats of the tabby weft, but these two blocks would look different than the other true crackle blocks in the finished cloth.

More than eight shafts. With more shafts, you get more blocks of crackle, and more design possibilities. Remember, the number of blocks possible equals the number of shafts available. I'll use 16-shaft crackle as an example, although I don't have a 16-shaft loom, so my designs are virtual, computer-only. First, design your block layout in a profile draft. Then use the tie-up ratio to determine the location of pattern, reverse-pattern, and background blocks relative to each other. You could certainly decide to have two pattern blocks, two reverse-pattern, and all the rest background. But imagine what else you could do with such a large design space. Pairs of pattern and reverse-pattern blocks could be next to each other or separated by background. You could have two pairs of pattern blocks in your design, one pair surrounded by reverse-pattern blocks, and one pair surrounded by background. The tie-up ratio 2/2/2/1/1/1/2/1/1/1, used for the pattern-only draft in *Figure 5-23*, makes that design. I have arranged the blocks in straight twill order, but imagine building curves with your blocks by varying their widths and heights. Or try arranging your blocks in advancing, broken, or other twill orders.

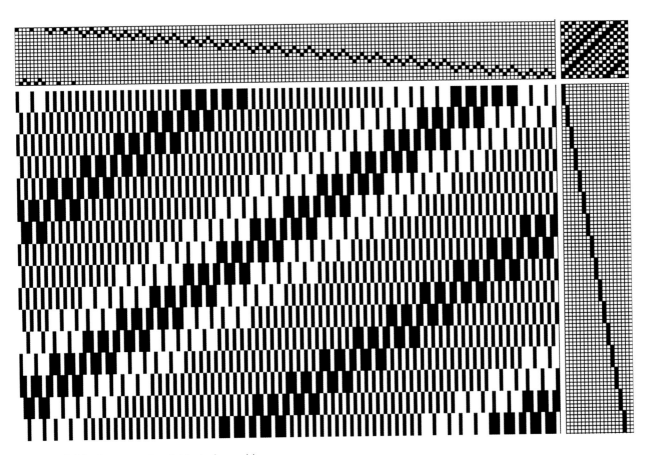

Figure 5-23. An example of 16-shaft crackle.

Design Considerations

Scale is a major design challenge with multi-shaft crackle. Designs with more blocks quickly get large and chunky looking. One way to reduce the scale is, of course, to use finer yarns. Another way is to thread and weave smaller blocks. You may have noticed that when blocks are only one repeat of the threading key wide and are threaded consecutively, crackle threading drafts look like advancing twill. The threadings are zigzag lines moving up or down at angles. Even when working with these small blocks, it is very helpful in understanding the draft to remember that crackle is a block weave. If you know where the blocks begin and end, and can identify the incidentals, you will find multi-shaft crackle with these small blocks much easier to design and thread. You will be less likely to make treadling errors if you keep block treadling sequences in mind as you weave.

Another technique to reduce the apparent scale of a design is to arrange your blocks in groups of four in the same or similar profiles. Look back at the pillow in *Figure 5-4* for an example. Here is the 8-block profile threading:

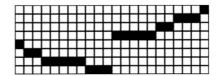

Treadling the blocks in straight order makes half-drop patterns. The scale of the overall design appears reduced, but all blocks are used. This is a technique that I use often and you will see more of later in the chapter.

I also like to break the blocks into smaller groups in the treadling, as seen previously in *Figure 5-7*. In that sample, blocks were threaded in a large point arrangement (Block A through H and back). I treadled four blocks in straight order, then skipped to the last block and treadled the remaining four blocks in reverse order. In *Figure 5-8* on the same warp, I reduced the scale of the design by treadling each block only one repeat of the key high, in advancing twill order. This produced a delicate lacy effect along the sides of the diamond motif.

Use profile drafting, our powerful design tool for block weaves, to make curves or other shapes. Profile drafting will give you the confidence to correctly insert an extra incidental as a design element in a wide block, as we saw in Chapter 2, *Figure 2-7*. Kaulitz (1994) recommends using any twill as a profile draft for crackle. Familiar twill patterns will appear larger in scale when crackle threading keys are substituted into profiles generated from twills. Griswold (2004) describes a similar process, designing on a "path," as a way of generating multi-shaft crackle patterns. The path is essentially a profile draft. A single threading key can be substituted into each square, or a motif or group of keys could be substituted. Substituting a sizeable motif, such as a group of four or five crackle keys in a broken order for example, along a path would greatly increase the scale of the design.

Treadling Variations

Classic crackle. The classic treadling on more than four shafts, with three different wefts, is rarely seen but produces fascinating effects. Look at the samples in *Figures 5-24* and *5-25* to see the variety in block structures of classic 6-shaft crackle woven with the two tie-ups I discussed earlier in the chapter. *Figure 5-24* illustrates the 2/2/1/1 tie-up and *5-25* shows the 1/2/2/1 tie-up. Warp is natural cotton, pattern weft is very dark green, and ground wefts are medium green and copper brown. One block, the darkest, is a pattern block and is structurally the same as in 4-shaft classic crackle. One is the same as "background" in classic 4-shaft crackle. The remaining four blocks are different from each other structurally and have unique color arrangements of pattern and ground wefts. Edges of the blocks are clean and distinct. The horizontal undulation is due to varying take-up in the six different block structures.

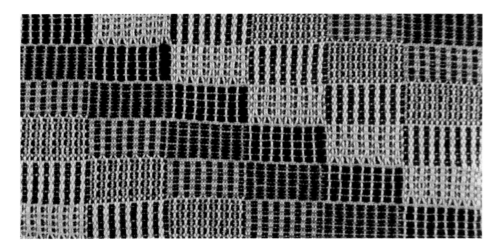

Figure 5-24. 6-shaft classic crackle sample, 2/2/1/1 tie-up.

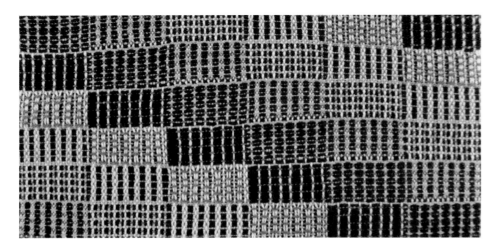

Figure 5-25. 6-shaft classic crackle sample, 1/2/2/1 tie-up.

The 6-shaft cotton classic crackle scarf in *Figure 5-26* has black warp and pattern weft and five colors of ground wefts rotated over the six blocks. What are those dashes of lime green that appear to weave in and out along the sides of the blocks? The incidentals! I enjoy adding an accent color in just the warp incidentals to give a little spark to a design.

Figure 5-26a. Detail.

Figure 5-26.
6-shaft classic
crackle scarf,
cotton.

With 8-shaft classic crackle the blocks are softer than those woven in the overshot manner. They seem almost blurry. *Figures 5-27, 5-28,* and *5-29* show samples of tie-ups *a, b,* and *c* discussed earlier in the chapter. With tie-ups *a* and *b*, we get two dark pattern blocks, two light reverse-pattern blocks, two true plain weave background blocks, and two transitional blocks where the ground wefts bleed out onto background. With tie-up *c*, in which pattern and reverse-pattern blocks are separated rather than adjacent, there are no longer any plain weave background blocks. The effect is even softer as ground wefts blend in and out across blocks.

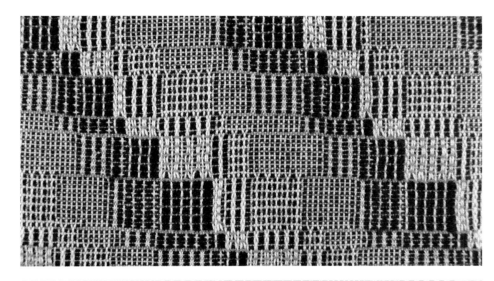

Figure 5-27.
8-shaft classic crackle sample, tie-up *a*.

Figure 5-28.
8-shaft classic crackle sample, tie-up *b*.

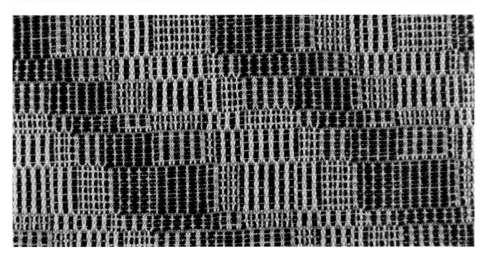

Figure 5-29.
8-shaft classic crackle sample, tie-up *c*.

The complete draft in *Figure 5-30* shows the structure of the fabric using tie-up **a**. In *5-31* and *5-32* are cloth diagrams of tie-up **b** and tie-up **c**, respectively. Treadling keys for 8-shaft classic crackle are:

Block A:	8 1 2 1 (8)
Block B:	1 2 3 2 (1)
Block C:	2 3 4 3 (2)
Block D:	3 4 5 4 (3)
Block E:	4 5 6 5 (4)
Block F:	5 6 7 6 (5)
Block G:	6 7 8 7 (6)
Block H:	7 8 1 8 (7)

Please note that upon further investigation, I have found that my original classic crackle treadling keys in *Weaver's* magazine (Issue 27, 1995) are indeed correct; the erratum published in Issue 32 is not correct after all. I erred in thinking I had erred in the first place!

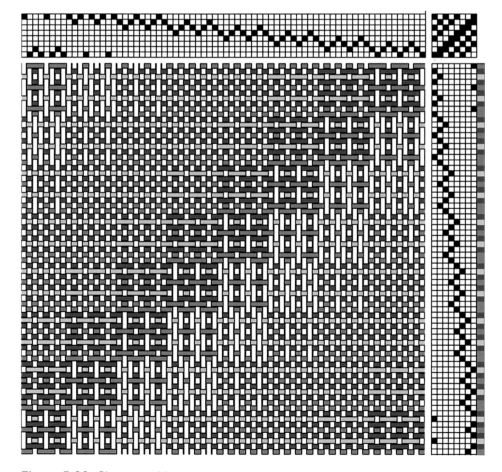

Figure 5-30. Classic crackle, tie-up **a**.

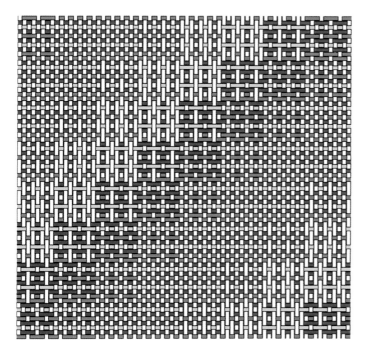

Figure 5-31. Classic crackle, tie-up *b*.

Figure 5-32. Classic crackle, tie-up *c*.

Classic crackle treadling gives us wonderful opportunity for color work with multi-shaft crackle. In *Figures 5-33* and *5-34* are two 8-shaft classic crackle scarves, woven with tie-ups *a* and *c* respectively. Blocks and colors are distinct and strong with tie-up *a*; with tie-up *c* they are blended and soft. Warp is light gray Tencel® lyocell, with dark red-orange incidentals for accent. Pattern weft is charcoal gray wool/silk. Ground wefts are tones of blue, green, and red. These scarves illustrate the design idea discussed earlier of combining groups of blocks into motifs to reduce the scale of the design.

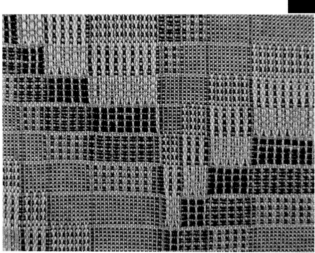

Figure 5-33a. Detail. Note the dark red-orange incidentals for accent.

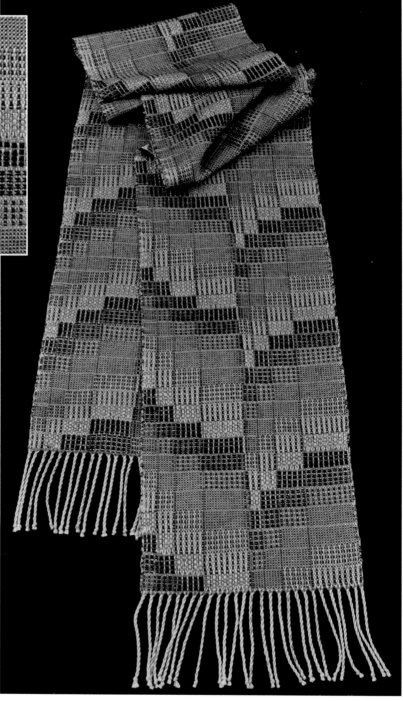

Figure 5-33.
Classic crackle scarf, Tencel® lyocell and wool/ silk blend, tie-up *a*.

Figure 5-34a. Detail.

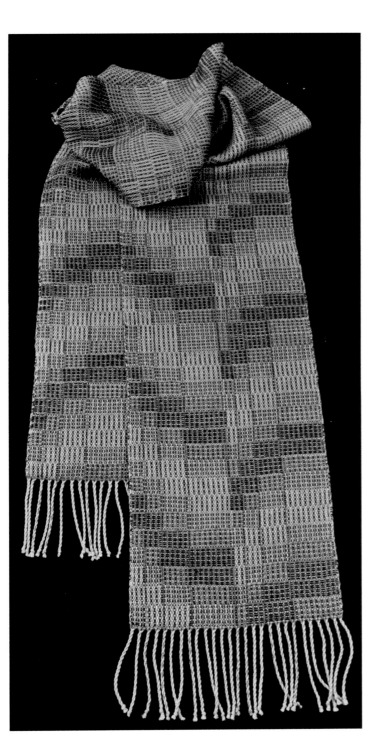

Figure 5-34.
Classic crackle scarf,
Tencel® lyocell and
wool/silk blend, tie-up **c**.

Another example of classic 8-shaft crackle is the silk scarf in *Figure 5-35*. A coral pattern weft and violet, blue and, blue-green ground wefts float on rose warp with gold incidentals for accent.

Figure 5-35a. Detail.

Figure 5-35.
Classic crackle
scarf, silk.

You may remember that I remarked in Chapter 2 that 4-shaft classic crackle with just one color weft was not particularly interesting. In contrast, because there are several different cloth structures in the eight classic crackle blocks, using just one weft on contrasting warp with 8-shaft crackle is lovely. It is especially effective with a striped or multi-color warp, as seen in the Tencel® lyocell scarves in *Figures 5-36* and *5-37*. The blocks shift between warp and weft emphasis, creating almost a painted warp effect.

Figure 5-37. Classic crackle scarf, Tencel® lyocell, black weft.

Figure 5-36.
Classic crackle scarf,
Tencel® lyocell, gray weft.

Treadled as summer & winter. Summer & winter treadlings, both paired and single, produce soft and shimmering effects on multi-shaft crackle. The 8-shaft samples in *Figures 5-38, 5-39,* and *5-40* are woven as paired summer & winter, using tie-ups *a*, *b*, and *c*. With tie-ups *a* and *b*, for each block treadling we get one true summer & winter pattern block, one true summer & winter background block (reverse-pattern), three intermediate or transitional blocks, and three blocks of near-plain weave background. The intermediate or half-tone block, which is similar to 4-shaft crackle woven summer & winter, is located between the pattern and reverse-pattern blocks. Two transitional blocks, one dark and one light, bleed out across background. With tie-up *c*, pattern and reverse-pattern are separated. Each has its own transitional blocks on either side. Background blocks are reduced to two. Treadling keys for 8-shaft crackle woven as paired summer & winter are:

Block A:	1 a 8 b 8 a 1 b
Block B:	2 a 1 b 1 a 2 b
Block C:	3 a 2 b 2 a 3 b
Block D:	4 a 3 b 3 a 4 b
Block E:	5 a 4 b 4 a 5 b
Block F:	6 a 5 b 5 a 6 b
Block G:	7 a 8 b 8 a 7 b
Block H:	8 a 7 b 7 a 8 b

Two of my crackle samples woven as paired summer & winter appear in Strickler (1991), one on the cover. In *Figure 5-41* is another sample not included in that book.

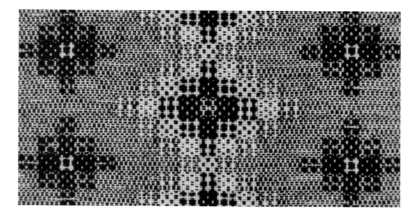

Figure 5-41.

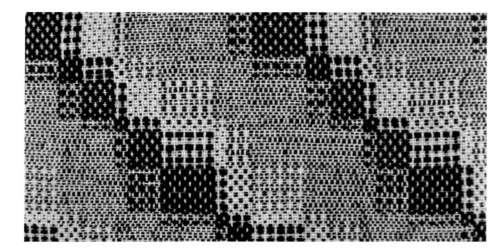

Figure 5-38.
Sample woven as paired
summer & winter, tie-up *a*.

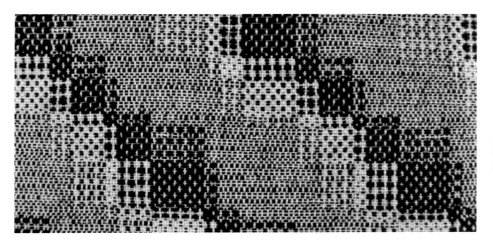

Figure 5-39.
Sample woven as paired
summer & winter, tie-up *b*.

Figure 5-40.
Sample woven as paired
summer & winter, tie-up *c*.

Traditional polychrome. Traditional polychrome, presented in Chapter 4, is easy to apply to crackle on more shafts. Treadling order is pattern color x, pattern color y on the next pattern treadle, tabby. In samples using tie-ups **a** and **b**, shown on opposite page in *Figures 5-42* and *5-43*, we get one pattern block and one background (reverse-pattern) block exactly like those in 4-shaft traditional polychrome crackle. An intermediate block is either one of the pattern colors or the other, depending on tie-up and color order in weaving. Then there are two other transitional blocks and three near-plain weave background blocks. With tie-up **c** *(Figure 5-44)*, which separates pattern and reverse-pattern blocks in the tie-up, background is reduced to one block and there are more transitional blocks. Treadling keys for these three tie-ups in traditional polychrome are:

Block A:	8 1 a 8 1 b
Block B:	1 2 a 1 2 b
Block C:	2 3 a 2 3 b
Block D:	3 4 a 3 4 b
Block E:	4 5 a 4 5 b
Block F:	5 6 a 5 6 b
Block G:	6 7 a 6 7 b
Block H:	7 8 a 7 8 b

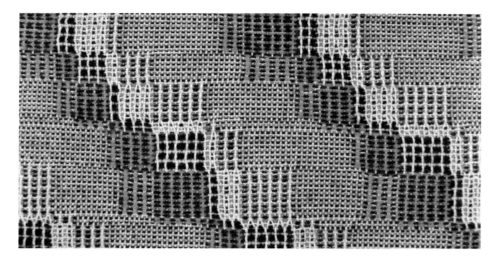

Figure 5-42.
Traditional polychrome
sample, tie-up *a*.

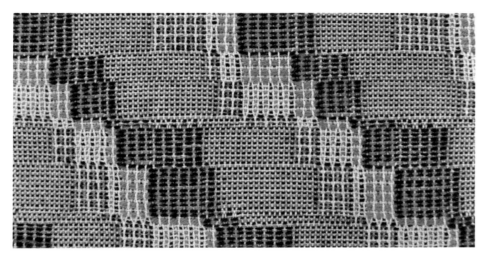

Figure 5-43.
Traditional polychrome
sample, tie-up *b*.

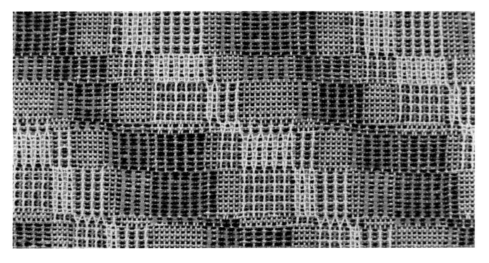

Figure 5-44.
Traditional polychrome
sample, tie-up *c*.

Then I wondered what would happen if I used tie-up **a** again, but separated the colors in the treadling. For example, if I wove pattern color *x* with Treadle 1, I would use Treadle 5 for color *y*, which is as far away as possible from 1 in either direction in the 1 through 8 order. This is treadling on opposites, with tabby between each pair of pattern wefts. *Figure 5-45* shows that effect. Colors are separated as much as possible from each other. There are no longer true pattern, reverse-pattern, or background blocks. Instead, there are various intermediate and transitional blocks, with more warp emphasis or more weft emphasis in one or both colors. Very interesting! Treadling keys for separated colors to use on either tie-up **a** or **b** are:

Block A:	1 5 a 1 5 b
Block B:	2 6 a 2 6 b
Block C:	3 7 a 3 7 b
Block D:	4 8 a 4 8 b
Block E:	5 1 a 5 1 b
Block F:	6 2 a 6 2 b
Block G:	7 3 a 7 3 b
Block H:	8 4 a 8 4 b

Figure 5-45. Traditional polychrome sample, tie-up **a**, colors separated in treadling.

Figure 5-46 shows a table runner in polychrome crackle woven using tie-up *a*, with pattern colors on adjacent treadles. Warp and tabby are natural linen; pattern wefts are taupe and light peach linen.

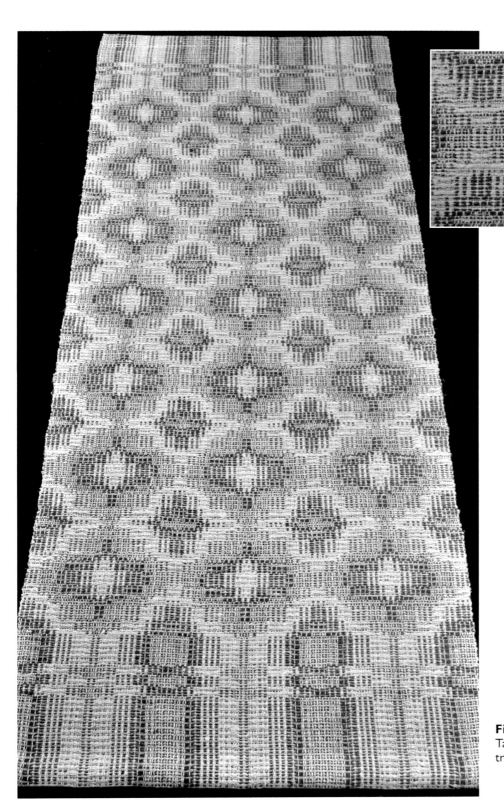

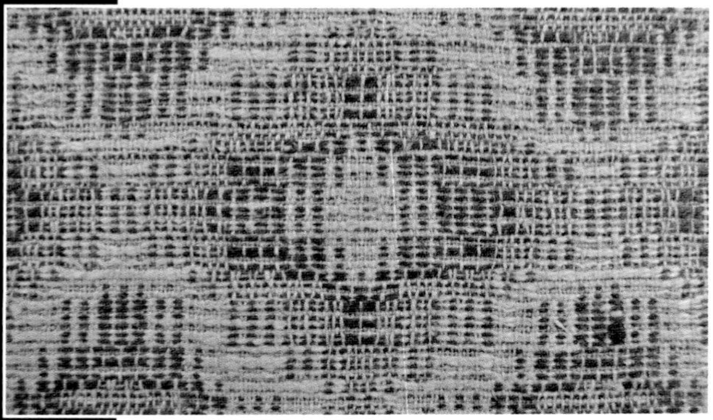

Figure 5-46a. Detail.

Figure 5-46.
Table runner, linen, woven traditional polychrome.

Lacy effects, Our lace treadlings from Chapter 3, Bronson, mystery, and two-block lace, all work well on multi-shaft crackle. In the 4-shaft versions, four different lace blocks and no plain weave were produced. With eight shafts, there are four lace blocks and four plain weave blocks. For treadling keys, simply extend the same keys given in Chapter 3 onto more shafts. Swatches of Bronson lace, mystery lace, and two-block lace treadlings woven with tie-up *a* are shown in *Figures 5-47, 5-48,* and *5-49*. In Bronson lace and mystery lace, the plain weave blocks have two or more wefts in the same shed where blocks change, making ribs. The ribs between the plain weave blocks can be eliminated in the Bronson lace treadling by reversing the tabby order in treadling keys. For example, treadle [b-pattern-b-pattern-b-a] instead of [a-pattern-a-pattern-a-b].

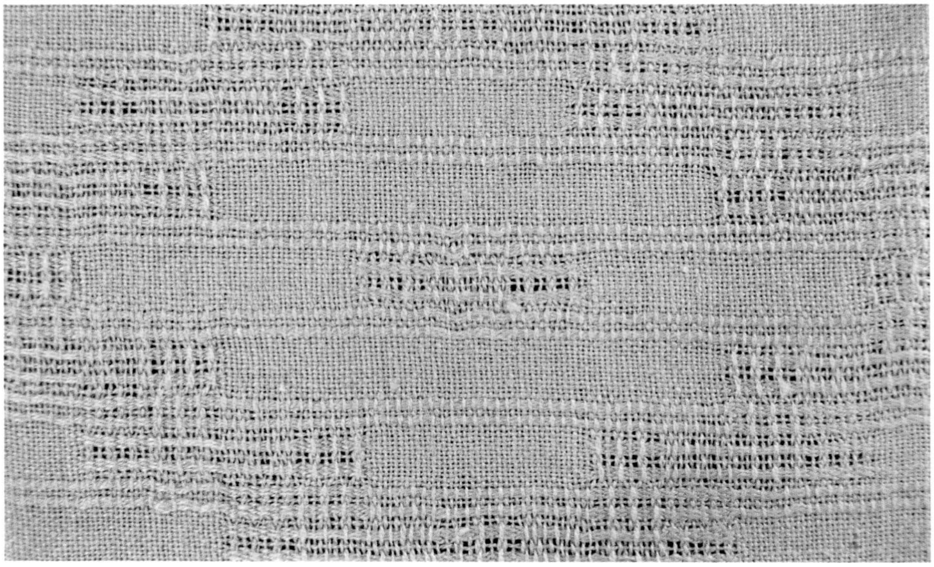

Figure 5-47. Sample treadled as Bronson lace, tie-up *a*.

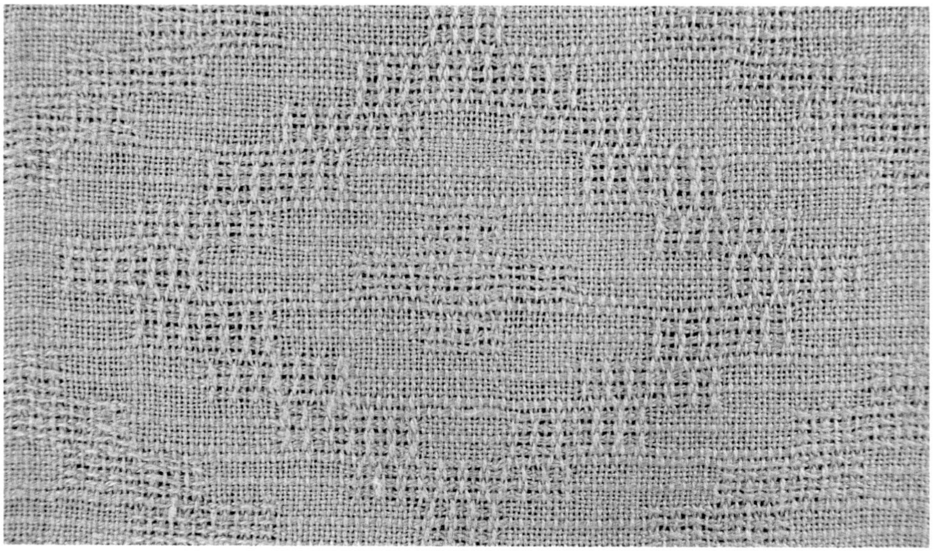

Figure 5-48.
Sample treadled as
mystery lace, tie-up *a*.

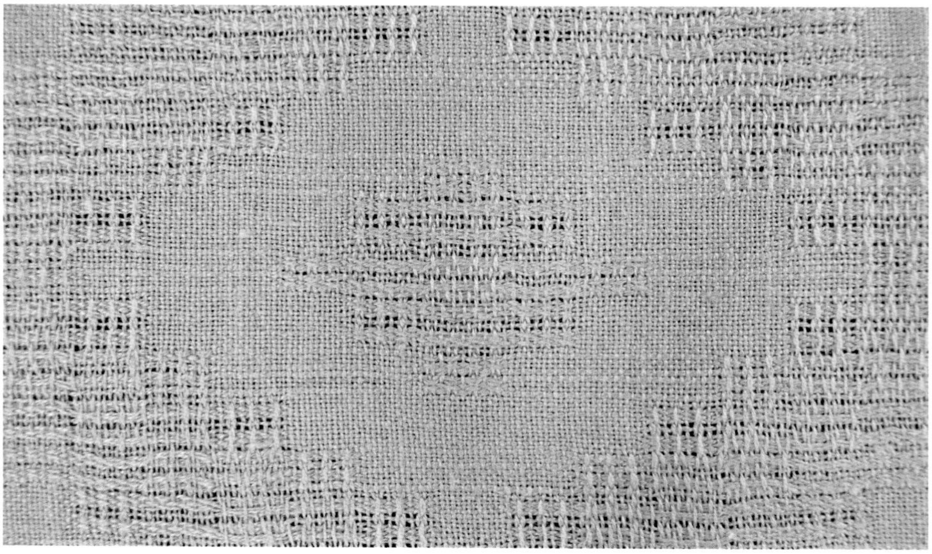

Figure 5-49.
Sample treadled as two-block lace, tie-up *a*.

Combining treadling methods in one piece is as effective with multi-shaft crackle as with four shafts. A mystery lace body is combined with a traditional polychrome border in the linen table runner in *Figure 5-50*. The polychrome was woven with tie-up *a*, pattern colors on adjacent treadles and without tabby. Because the tie-up contains four blocks of plain weave, generally multi-shaft polychrome crackle is structurally stable without tabby.

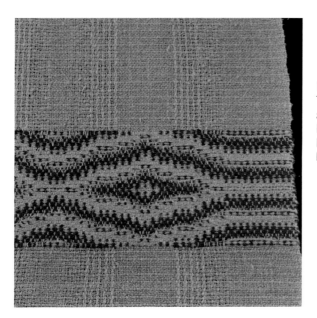

Figure 5-50.
Table runner, linen and linen /rayon blend, mystery lace body, polychrome border.

Petitpoint swivel. Petitpoint swivel treadling on 8-shaft crackle is delightful, but has some challenges in designing and treadling. You can see in *Figure 5-51* that, just as in 4-shaft petitpoint, we get one pattern block with dense dots of color and two intermediate half-tone blocks. All the remaining blocks are plain weave background. Where is the pattern weft in those blocks? As you would predict, it is floating across the back of the cloth until it is needed to make pattern on the front again. Depending on the width of the blocks, those floats could be very long (*Figure 5-52*).

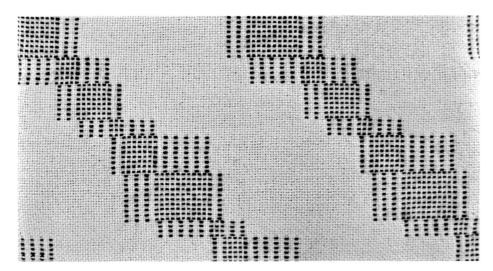

Figure 5-51. Sample treadled as petitpoint swivel.

Figure 5-52. Long floats on back.

To weave petitpoint crackle we need an unbalanced tie-up. In order to get enough treadles and not make the lift combinations too heavy, we'll use a skeleton tie-up. Here is the tie-up:

1	2	3	4	5	6	7	8	a	b
8		8		8					8
	7		7				7	7	
6		6				6			6
	5				5		5	5	
4				4		4			4
		3		3			3	3	
	2		2		2				2
	1		1		1			1	

Step on two treadles at once to get the combinations for pattern shafts. Weave the first pick with pattern weft, followed by two picks with ground weft in same yarn as warp. Treadling keys are:

Block A:	I+a a b
Block B:	2+b b a
Block C:	3+a a b
Block D:	4+b b a
Block E:	5+a a b
Block F:	6+b b a
Block G:	7+a a b
Block H:	8+b b a

What else could we do with those long floats across five plain weave background blocks? One idea (*Figure 5-53*) is to clip the floats to make fringe or "eyelashes" on the sides of blocks.

Figure 5-53.

Another possibility is to put another set of pattern and half-tone blocks with a second pattern color into the background, making polychrome petitpoint swivel, as in *Figure 5-54*. Treadle the first pattern color as in the treadling keys above. Then weave a second pattern color, stepping on the treadle farthest away in both directions, plus the same tabby treadle as in the first shot. Follow with same tabby and other tabby with ground weft. Treadling keys are:

Block A:	1+a 5+a a b
Block B:	2+b 6+b b a
Block C:	3+a 7+a a b
Block D:	4+b 8+b b a
Block E:	5+a 1+a a b
Block F:	6+b 2+b b a
Block G:	7+a 3+a a b
Block H:	8+b 4+b b a

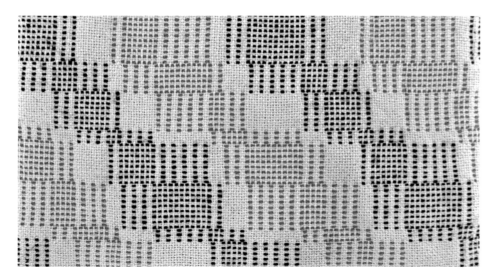

Figure 5-54. Polychrome petitpoint swivel sample.

For comparison of several treadling variations, I wove a series of table runners on a black linen warp all with the same block order and heights. I used tie-up **c**, which separates the pattern and reverse-pattern blocks in the tie-up. Tabby is black and pattern wefts are grayed blue-green and/or red. *Figure 5-55* is woven as overshot and *5-56* as single summer & winter. Polychrome is in *Figure 5-57*. *Figure 5-58* shows polychrome with tie-up **a** and pattern colors separated in treadling.

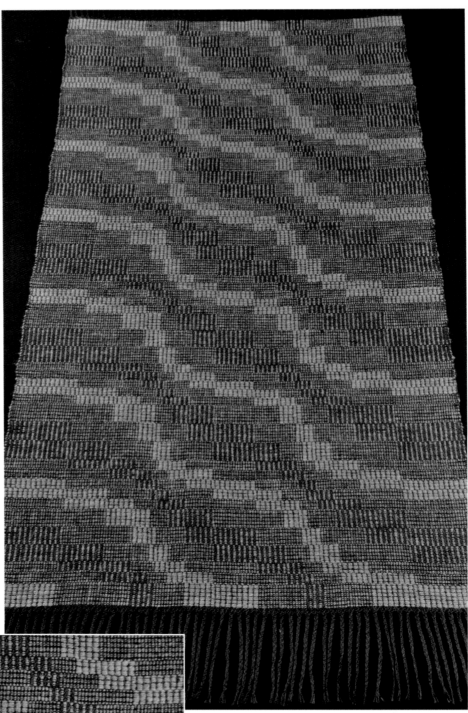

Figure 5-55.
Table runner, linen and linen/cotton/rayon blend, woven as overshot, tie-up **c**.

Figure 5-55a.
Detail.

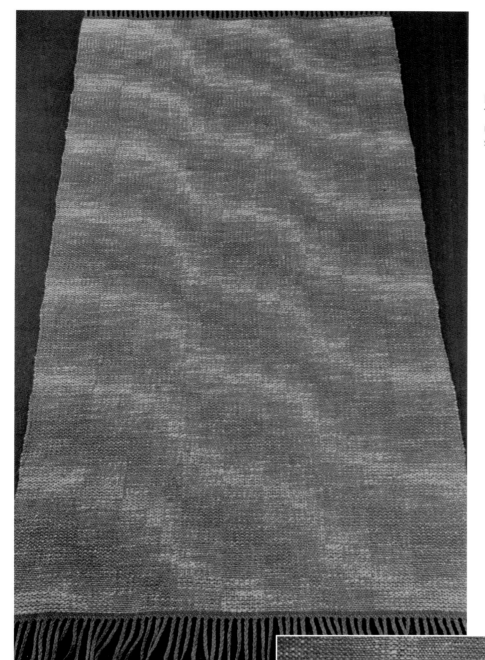

Figure 5-56.
Table runner, linen/cotton/
rayon blend, woven as single
summer & winter, tie-up **c**.

Figure 5-56a.
Detail.

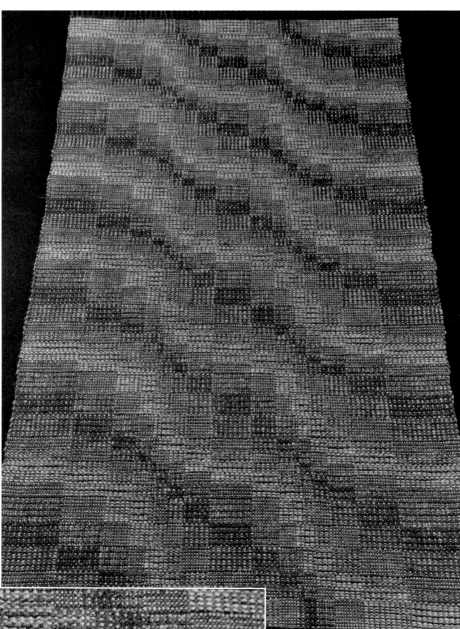

Figure 5-57.
Table runner, linen/cotton/rayon blend, woven as traditional polychrome, tie-up **c**.

Figure 5-57a.
Detail.

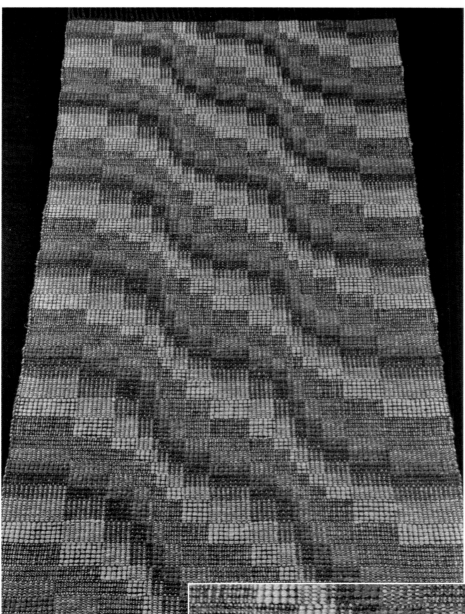

Figure 5-58.
Table runner, linen/cotton/rayon blend, woven as traditional polychrome, tie-up *a*, colors separated in treadling.

Figure 5-58a.
Detail.

In conclusion, with multi-shaft crackle you can create fabrics that really are not as complex as they look. Crackle is a block weave. Use profile drafting for easy designing. Crackle's block keys help you keep your place when threading and weaving. Although you are working with rectangular design elements, the designs do not have to be blocky-looking. You can make curves with your blocks. Edges can be softened with a variety of alternate treadlings.

Chapter **6**
Even More with Crackle

Turned Crackle

Turning a draft is a technique that weavers often use to allow us to weave structures that require multiple shuttles with just one shuttle. What was the threading is now in the treadling, and what was treadling is now threading. Sometimes, turned drafts allow us to use fewer treadles as well.

Turning classic crackle. Classic crackle is woven as-drawn-in. Threading and treadling keys are identical structurally. To "turn" classic crackle, no manipulation of the draft is needed. Simply move the yarns that would have been pattern and ground wefts to their corresponding positions in the warp. Don't forget the incidentals. Move the warp yarns to the weft. If your original plan called for all the same yarn in the warp, then you can now weave classic crackle with one shuttle. A 4-shaft example is illustrated in *Figures 6-1* and *6-2* seen on following page.

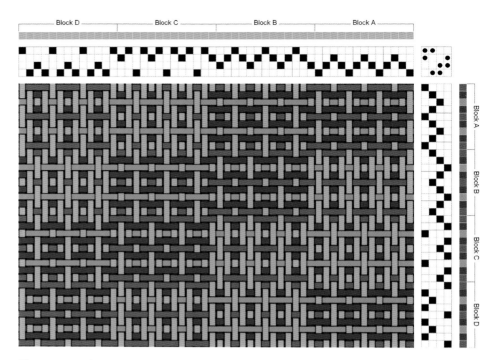

Figure 6-1. Classic crackle.

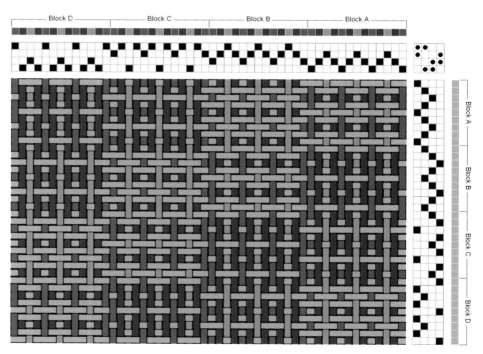

Figure 6-2. Turned classic crackle.

Turning classic crackle has the advantage of weaving with one shuttle rather than three. But, in order to put the colors in the warp, all the color decisions need to be made in advance. One of the exciting aspects of weaving crackle in the classic manner is being able to change the ground weft colors throughout the piece. This freedom to design at the loom is lost when colors are moved to the warp. *Figure 6-3* shows a scarf in "turned" classic crackle. The pattern warp is a highly textured boucle silk in a salmon color. There are four colors of fine silk ground warps: blue, turquoise, green, and rose. Only two colors are used in each block. Weft is fine lavender wool. Blocks are threaded in straight A-B-C-D order and treadled in broken order.

Figure 6-3a. Detail.

Figure 6-3.
Turned classic crackle scarf, silk and wool.

Turning crackle woven as overshot. Turning a draft in which the threading and treadling are not the same involves physical manipulation of the draft, as illustrated in *Figures 6-4* and *6-5*. To turn the draft in *6-4*, rotate the threading draft one-quarter turn clockwise. The threading is now vertical rather than horizontal, and becomes the treadling. Also turn the treadling one-quarter turn clockwise, and place it in the threading. To turn the tie-up, rotate it one-quarter turn clockwise. Then change the tie-up so that the blank squares are tied up, and the tied squares are left blank. Examine the draft in *6-5* to see how all the elements have been turned. Overshot treadling required six treadles; the turned draft now requires six shafts.

Because more shafts are required, turning crackle woven as overshot may not be useful for you. Also, we are accustomed to weaving with two shuttles, pattern alternating with tabby, so weaving with one shuttle may not be much of a time saver. If you have planned many color changes in the weft, however, it may be more convenient to have the color changes in the warp. You may prefer the look of vertical rather than horizontal stripes.

The principles of turning a draft can be applied to other treadling variations on crackle, and may be worth exploring. Of particular interest might be those treadlings that use multiple shuttles, such as the various polychrome methods.

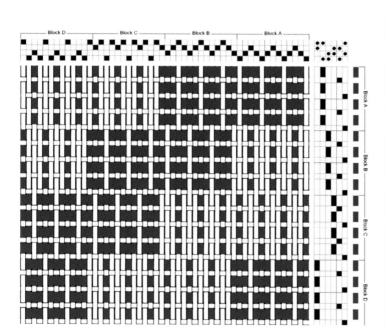

Figure 6-4. Crackle treadled as overshot.

Figure 6-5. Turned crackle, overshot treadling moved to threading.

Color-and-Weave Effects

Color-and-weave effects are repeating patterns created by alternation of contrasting colors both in the warp and in the weft. These alternating colors interact with the weave structure to create pattern in which the actual structure of the cloth is not always evident. Usually we see color-and-weave effects on plain weave or twill, but they can be very interesting when applied to other weave structures.

In color-and-weave notation, contrasting colors are usually referred to as "dark" and "light," although the contrast may be in hue, sheen, texture, or another yarn characteristic. Value contrasts produce the strongest color-and-weave effects. Color alternation can be done in various sequences, such as one dark alternated with one light, two dark and two light, three light and one dark. Common notation is "1D/1L" for the alternation of one dark and one light.

Four-shaft crackle. Let's see what happens when we make color-and-weave effects on crackle. *Figure 6-6* shows classic crackle with a 1D/1L color alternation in both warp and weft. In *Figure 6-7* the colors are 2D/2L in both warp and weft; *Figure 6-8* is 2D/2L in warp and 1D/3L in weft. Note that the crackle blocks are less distinct in the last two color orders, where the 2D/2L and 1D/3L weft alternations color changes do not correspond to block

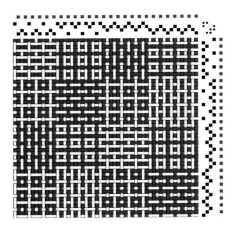

Figure 6-6. 1D/1L, classic crackle.

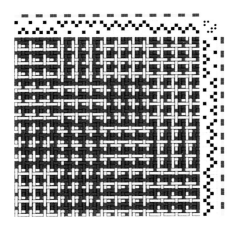

Figure 6-7. 2D/2L, classic crackle.

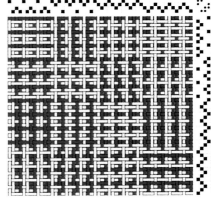

Figure 6-8. 2D/2L warp and 1D/3L weft, classic crackle.

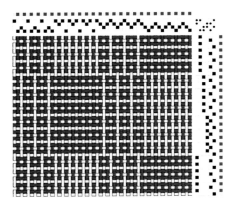

Figure 6-9. 1D/1L, overshot treadling.

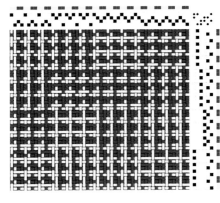

Figure 6-10. 2D/2L, overshot treadling.

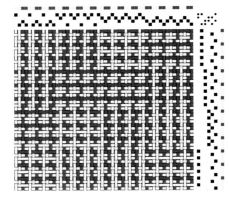

Figure 6-11. 2D/2L warp and 1D/3L weft, overshot treadling.

changes. In the 1D/1L alternation, because of the incidentals, color orders change from dark-light to light-dark in every other block. Blocks are clear, and there are eight color-and-weave patterns created with just four blocks of crackle. When the fabric is off the loom and finished, we can expect it to look quite different as the yarns move out of the rigid grid and pattern wefts pair together.

Figures 6-9, 6-10, and 6-11 show how the same color orders look when woven in the overshot manner. Interestingly, in 6-9, both Block B and Block C treadlings produce the same color-and-weave effects within the blocks. Blocks A and D also produce the same effects. Blocks are quite obscured with the second two color orders, as in the classic crackle drafts below.

Another way to produce color-and-weave effects on classic crackle is to assign "dark" or "light" specifically to pattern, ground weft x, and ground weft y. Figures 6-12 through 6-15 shows four samples of this type of color-and-weave treadling on a warp threaded 1D/1L.

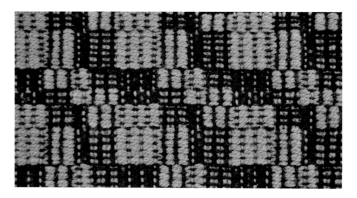

Figure 6-12. Light pattern, dark ground x, dark y.

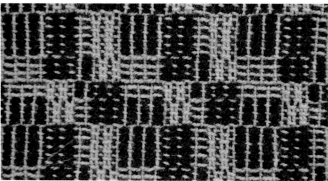

Figure 6-13. Dark pattern, light ground x, light y.

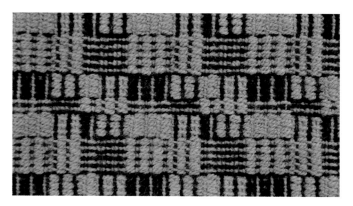

Figure 6-14. Light pattern, dark ground x, light y.

Figure 6-15. Dark pattern, light ground x, dark y.

Eight-shaft crackle. With eight blocks, three basic tie-ups, and many possible color orders in both threading and treadling, color-and-weave on 8-shaft crackle can create a myriad of patterns. You could make a very large gamp to sample color-and-weave and still not exhaust the possibilities. To give you a taste, *Figures 6-16* and *6-17* show two samplers with just a few combinations. Both samplers are threaded 1D/1L with eight crackle blocks in straight A through H order. In Chapter 5, *Figures 5-9, 5-10,* and *5-11,* I presented three tie-ups (*a, b,* and *c*) for 8-shaft crackle. Tie-up *b* was used for the color-and-weave sampler in *Figure 6-16* and tie-up *c* for sampler *6-17.* The top four samples in each sampler are woven in the overshot manner. From the top of the samplers, weft color orders are 1D/3L, 3D/1L, 2D/2L, and 1D/1L. In both samplers, the bottom sample is treadled classic crackle in 1D/1L color order. In classic crackle, thirteen different color-and-weave patterns appear in the blocks when tie-up *b* was used. Sixteen different patterns appear with tie-up *c.*

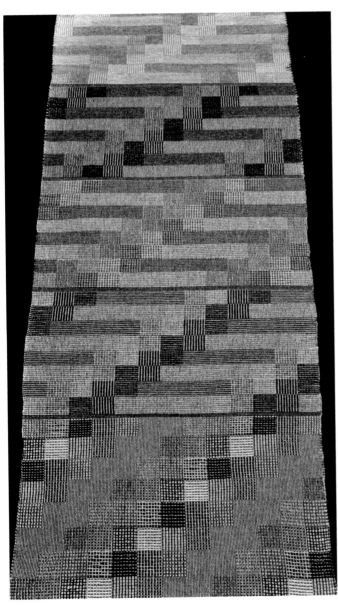

Figure 6-16.

Figure 6-17.

The draft in *Figure 6-18* illustrates 8-shaft classic crackle threaded and treadled 1D/1L with tie-up **c**. See if you can identify all sixteen different color-and-weave patterns. It may be difficult to spot them all in this drawdown, because it's hard to see the interlacements at such a small scale.

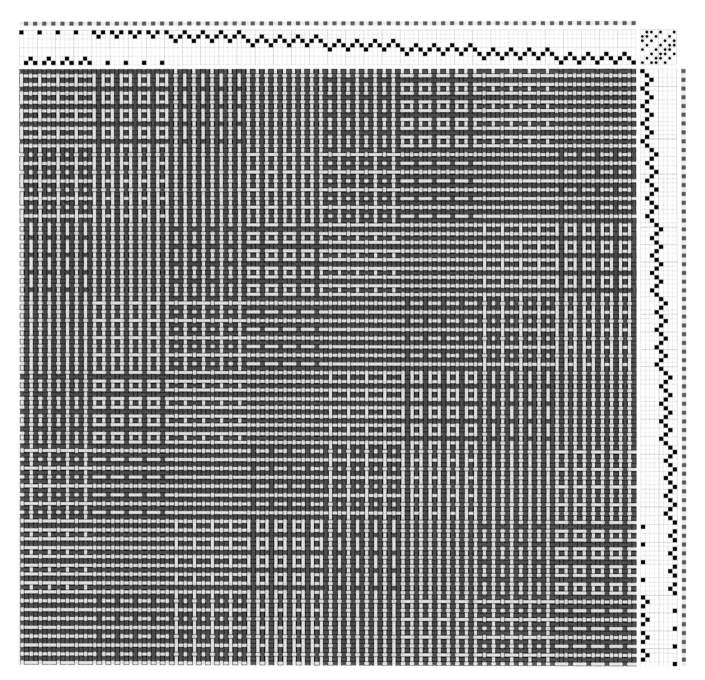

Figure 6-18. 8-shaft classic crackle, 1D/1L color-and-weave effect, tie-up **c**.

Eight Blocks on Four Shafts

If you have only four shafts, but want the look of more blocks in crackle, Zielinski (1981) gives us a way to push crackle to yield more blocks on fewer shafts. I suggest you read Zielinski's detailed account of how to derive the threading keys, but here is a summary.

Development of block threading keys. First, start by writing a threading draft for 4-shaft straight twill, leaving every other square on the graph paper blank, designated by = symbols in *Figure 6-19*. Although Zielinski's drafts read left-to-right, I have written the threading right-to-left, which is more customary in the United States. Then fill in the blank squares with a parallel straight twill one step back in the 1-2-3-4 twill order (+ symbols in *Figure 6-19*). For example, the first end is on Shaft 1, the first parallel end is on Shaft 4, which is behind 1 in the twill order. Shaft 2 is followed by 1, and so on.

Figure 6-19. Zielinski's block derivation.

Now identify all the different pairs of warp ends in the draft, reading from right to left, and including the last end of one pair in the next pair. The first pair is 1-4, then next pair is 4-2, then 2-1, followed by 1-3, 3-2, 2-4, 4-3, and wrapping around to the beginning, 3-1. Shafts 1 and 3 and Shafts 2 and 4 are paired twice but listed only once, leaving six different pairs. Because I am reading right to left, my pairs are in a different order than Zielinski's, but will yield the same combinations when re-written in numerical order: 1-4, 2-4, 1-2, 1-3, 2-3, and 3-4.

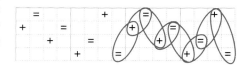

Then, to make 4-end threading keys with blocks that share ends or overlap as in standard crackle, combine two pairs together in all possible combinations. We end up with eight 4-end combinations. To convert these 4-end combinations into crackle-like threading keys, in which the second and fourth ends in each key are on the same shaft, Zielinski arrived at the following threading keys (after "a lot of paperwork" according to him):

Block A:	1 4 2 4 (1)
Block B:	4 2 1 2 (4)
Block C:	2 1 3 1 (2)
Block D:	1 3 2 3 (1)
Block E:	3 2 4 2 (3)
Block F:	2 4 3 4 (2)
Block G:	4 3 1 3 (4)
Block H:	3 1 4 1 (3)

None of these keys is exactly the same as a standard crackle key. Incidentals to complete a block, shown in parentheses, are on the same shaft that started the block. And remember, Zielinski's work was done with pencil and graph paper in the days before weave drafting software!

The tie-up. Zielinski gives us a tie-up with six pattern treadles, arranged in "walking" order. These six treadles are the same six treadles in our standard 2/2 tie-up, although treadles tied to 1-3 and 2-4 are now considered pattern treadles, not tabby. It is not possible to weave plain weave across all blocks on this new threading as the threading no longer alternates odd and even shafts. A pattern-only draft of Zielinski's eight crackle-like blocks is shown in *Figure 6-20*. Blocks are threaded and treadled in A through H order, along a diagonal so that they can be easily identified. The drawdown depicts only pattern wefts. Warp is white and pattern wefts are black. For consistency in this book, I have used the standard tie-up in the conventional order given in Chapter 2, rather than Zielinski's walking order.

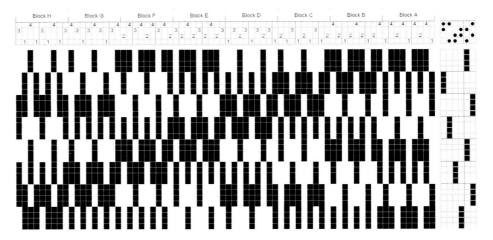

Figure 6-20. Zielinski's eight "crackle" blocks on four shafts.

We can see that many of the characteristics of true crackle are retained in this unusual draft. Blocks are not independent of each other. Two adjacent blocks weave pattern together. There are no weft floats longer than three ends, with 2-end floats where adjacent blocks join. With this new threading, though, there are indeed eight blocks on just four shafts. Treadles 1, 2, 3, and 4 each produce two pattern blocks, two background blocks, and four half-tone blocks. Treadles 5 and 6 each weave pattern in two pairs of blocks and background in two pairs of blocks, no half-tones. They are used twice in the sequence to make sure all eight threaded blocks appear on the diagonal.

Treadling methods. How do we weave this new 8-block "crackle"? Treadling does present some challenges. As Zielinski notes, we cannot weave in the usual overshot manner, pattern alternating with tabby, because plain weave is not possible. He gave us four treadling possibilities, but did not include drafts or photos of actual woven samples in his book. Zielinski also didn't comment on weft colors. To see how his suggested treadlings worked, I wove samples of all four treadlings on a natural cotton warp with dark green pattern weft and natural cotton ground weft (called a "binder" by Zielinski). All of the treadlings have an irregular, makeshift look in both pattern and background blocks.

The first treadling (*Figure 6-21*) is woven on opposites, using the opposite shed to the pattern shed as a binder. A second method, shown in *Figure 6-22*, alternates pattern on one treadle with binders on each of the other treadles in order, for example [1(pattern)-2(binder)-1-3-1-4-1-5-1-6]. This treadling produces 5-pick warp floats in some of the blocks. At times float lengths vary within the same block. Binder wefts tend to slide around in the longer warp float areas, creating unusual patterns and a rather untidy overall look.

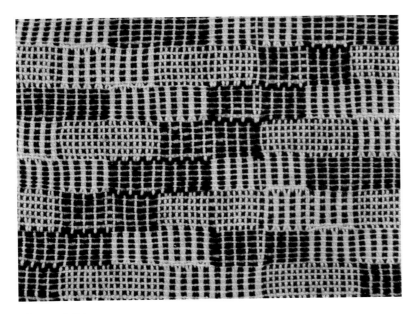

Figure 6-21.

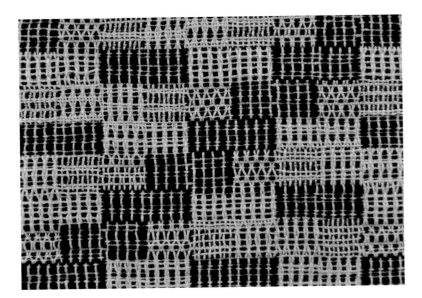

Figure 6-22.

Zielinski describes a third treadling option, alternating pattern with two binders on a pair of opposite treadles that does not include the pattern treadle *(Figure 6-23)*. An example is [1 (pattern)-2 (binder)-1 (pattern)-4 (binder)]. Or you could use Treadles 5 and 6 as binders with pattern on Treadle 1. Float lengths remain consistent with this treadling, but using just one ground weft the same color as the warp does not produce a particularly interesting fabric. A fourth method *(Figure 6-24)* suggested by Zielinski is to alternate three other treadles with pattern, the first treadle opposite to pattern and the other two a different pair of opposites, for example [1(pattern)-3(binder)-1-5-1-6]. As in the third method, no floats are longer than three ends. Pattern wefts are not consistently paired as in the third treadling, however. Instead, they alternate between paired and single, and tend to look like treadling errors.

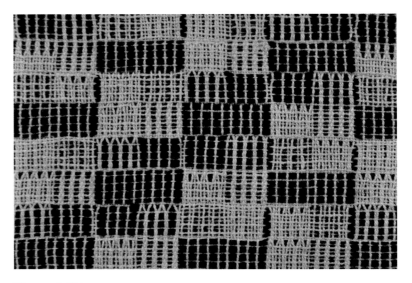

Figure 6-23.

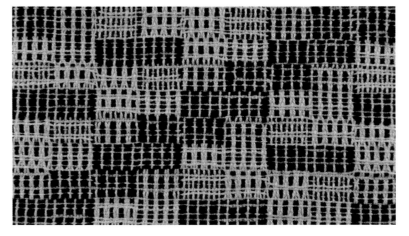

Figure 6-24.

Polychrome treadlings on Zielinski's eight blocks were more successful. Using the third treadling method and alternating two colors in the binders, the sample in *Figure 6-25* looks very much like 4-shaft classic crackle, including a few "crackles." But there are indeed eight blocks. On the natural cotton warp, dark green pattern blocks align along the diagonal. Binders, or ground wefts, are turquoise and red. There are eight different color effects in the eight blocks. Colors seem to move around in unpredictable ways, creating a "modernistic" look. Experiment with which of the two pairs of opposites to use with each pattern treadle to get the color effect you want. For *6-25*, I re-ordered the treadling keys to be more like classic crackle keys, leading with ground (binder) x, then pattern, then ground (binder) y, then pattern, and ending the block with an incidental ground (binder) x. My treadling keys for *6-25* are:

Block A:	1 5 3 5 (1)
Block B:	5 1 6 1 (5)
Block C:	2 6 4 6 (2)
Block D:	5 2 6 2 (5)
Block E:	1 5 3 5 (1)
Block F:	5 3 6 3 (5)
Block G:	2 6 4 6 (2)
Block H:	5 4 6 4 (5)

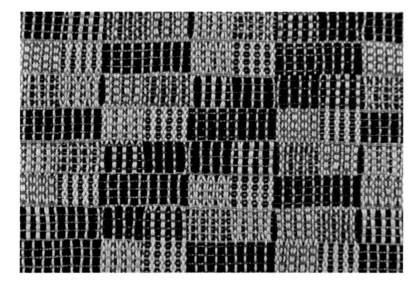

Figure 6-25.

Using three different colors in the binders in Zielinski's fourth method (*Figure 6-26*) might be worth further exploration. In that sample, binders are red, turquoise, and yellow-green. With more colors, somehow the inconsistency in pairing of pattern wefts seems less distracting than it was in *6-24*. These treadling repeats are not easy to follow, though, and are even more difficult with several shuttles. As with all of Zielinski's treadlings, careful sampling is recommended!

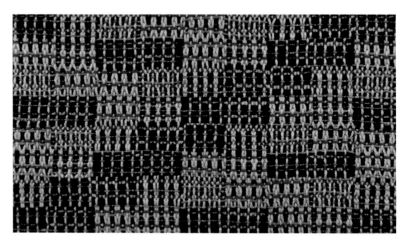

Figure 6-26.

Conclusion

 As we have seen throughout the book, crackle's makeshift nature makes it ideal for pushing in new directions. Four-shaft crackle woven in the classic manner in Chapter 2 has great potential for color work. An amazing array of very different fabrics can be produced with many unusual treadling methods presented in Chapters 3 and 4. Chapter 5 showed that crackle on more than four may be more complex, but not necessarily better, just different. Some ideas for even further exploration of this versatile structure were presented in Chapter 6. I hope you will enjoy experimenting with crackle as much as I have over the years.

Glossary

3-shaft point twill – a twill that is threaded on three shafts and reverses direction of the diagonal at a point, for example 1-2-3-2-1-2-3-2.

as drawn in – treadled exactly as threaded. Can also refer to block order treadled as threaded.

block weave – a weave structure that creates designs composed of rectangles of contrasting effects, for example pattern rectangles vs. background rectangles.

Bronson lace – a lace block weave that produces two blocks on four shafts. Blocks are independent and can be plain weave or lace.

gamp – a sampler of certain effects (such as color, value, pattern) where the effects are threaded and treadled in sections, showing interaction of each threading with each treadling.

incidentals – extra warp ends or weft picks inserted in a crackle draft to complete blocks and maintain the odd-even progression in threading or treadling.

overshot – a twill-based block weave that produces four blocks on four shafts. Designs are created by small pattern, background, and half-tone blocks. Supplementary pattern wefts alternate with tabby and float across the full width of the block.

pattern-only draft – a structural draft that shows only the pattern wefts, although tabby or ground wefts may be used in treadling.

profile draft – a design draft that depicts the layout, positions, and sizes of blocks and can be interpreted in various weave structures.

skeleton tie-up – a tie-up that requires stepping on two treadles at once, used when there are not enough treadles to tie up all the needed shaft lift combinations.

structural draft – a complete draft that gives all information needed for threading and tying up the loom, and weaving the cloth. A cloth diagram shows the exact thread-by-thread cloth structure.

summer & winter – a tied block weave that produces two blocks (pattern and background) on four shafts. Blocks are independent. Supplementary pattern wefts alternate with tabby and are tied down by every fourth warp end.

threading key – a sequence of warp ends that is repeated to create a block of desired width.

treadling key – a sequence of weft picks that is repeated to create a block of desired height.

twill tie-up ratio – a series of numbers alternating above and below a horizontal line indicating how treadles are tied up.

twill-based block weave – a block weave with threading and treadling keys that are twill sequences.

unit weave – a block weave with blocks that are independent of each other, do not share pattern shafts in common, and can be combined at will in designing.

Bibliography

 For your convenience, I have placed references in four categories based on their primary content. Some references are listed in more than one section.

Drafting and Designing Crackle

Atwater, Mary M. *Shuttle-Craft Bulletin.* Cambridge, Massachusetts and Basin, Montana: Shuttle-Craft Guild, 1927-1946. (Whole issues on crackle in August 1936, July 1938, and August 1941).

_____. *The Shuttle-Craft Book of American Hand-Weaving.* New York: Macmillan, 1928. Reprint, Coupeville, Washington: HTH Publishers, 1986.

_____. "Notes on the Crackle Weave." *Practical Weaving Suggestions,* Shelby, North Carolina: Lily Mills, vol.2, date unknown.

_____. *The Crackle Weave: Patterns and Notes Prepared for the Shuttle-Craft Guild.* Basin, Montana: Shuttle-Craft Guild, 1930.

Barrett, Clotilde. "Crackle." *The Weaver's Journal,* January 1979.

Black, Mary. *The Key to Weaving.* New York: Macmillan, 1945. Reprint, 1980.

Douglas, Harriet C. *Handweaver's Instruction Manual.* Santa Ana, California: HTH Publishers, 1949.

_____. *The Shuttle-Craft Guild Bulletin.* Basin, Montana: Shuttle-Craft Guild, 1949.

Frey, Berta. *Designing and Drafting for Handweavers.* New York: Macmillan, 1958. Reprint, New York: Collier, 1975.

Getzmann, Ulla. *Weave Structures the Swedish Way: Book 1.* Translated and adapted by Becky Ashenden. Shelburne, Massachusetts: Väv Stuga Press, 2006.

Griswold, Ralph E. "Crackle Weave, Part 1: Designing with Blocks and Motifs." 2004. http://www.cs.arizona.edu/patterns/weaving/webdocs.

_____. "Crackle Weave, Part 2: Tie-ups and Treadlings." 2004. http://www.cs.arizona.edu/patterns/weaving/webdocs.

_____. "Crackle Weave, Part 3: Path Design." 2004. http://www.cs.arizona.edu/patterns/weaving/webdocs.

Hutchison, Jean and Caryl Sedushak. *Let's Tackle Crackle.* Self-published, 1999.

Kaulitz, Manuela. "Crackle Patterns from Twill Profiles."*Handwoven*, September/October 1994.

Moes, Dini. "Crackle Weave." *Shuttle Spindle & Dyepot,* Winter 1993.

Peters, Rupert. "Some Notes on Crackle Weave."*Practical Weaving Suggestions,* Shelby, North Carolina: Lily Mills, vol.2, 1957.

Snyder, Mary E. *The Crackle Weave.* Avon, Connecticut: Book Barn, 1961.

Thorpe, Heather G. *A Handweaver's Workbook.* New York: Macmillan, 1956.

Tidball, Harriet. *The Handloom Weaves: Shuttlecraft Guild Monograph 33.* Freeland, Washington: HTH Publishers, 1957.

_____. *The Weaver's Book: Fundamentals of Handweaving.* New York: Macmillan, 1961.

Wilson, Susan. "Classic Crackle." *Weaver's* 22, 1993.

_____. "Crackle Weave." *Shuttle Spindle & Dyepot,* Winter 2001.

Zielinski, S.A. *Contemporary Approach to Traditional Weaves: Crackle, M's&O's and Others,* Master Weaver Library Volume 8. L'Islet, Québec, Canada: Nilus Leclerc, Inc., 1981.

Treadling Variations

Atwater, Mary M. "Notes on the Crackle Weave." *Practical Weaving Suggestions,* Shelby, North Carolina: Lily Mills, vol.2, date unknown.

Barrett, Clotilde. *Summer and Winter and Beyond: Weaver's Journal Monograph Two.* Boulder, Colorado: Colorado Fiber Center, Inc., 1979.

_____. "Crackle." *The Weaver's Journal,* January 1979.

_____. "Swivel Explored and Contradicted." *The Weaver's Journal,* April 1979.

Blau, Ruth. "Color Sequencing in Polychrome Crackle Blocks." *Complex Weavers Journal*, September 2003.

Blum, Grace D. *Functional Overshot.* West Chicago, Illinois: Grace D. Blum, 1960.

Bress, Helene. *The Weaving Book: Patterns and Ideas.* New York: Scribner's, 1981.

Griffin, Gertrude, ed. "Polychrome." *The Tie-Up*, newsletter of the Southern California Handweavers' Guild 21, 1971.

Hoskins, Nancy Arthur. *Weft-Faced Pattern Weaves: Tabby to Taquete.* Seattle, Washington: University of Washington Press, 1992.

Hutchison, Jean and Caryl Sedushak. *Let's Tackle Crackle.* Self-published, 1999.

Lermond, Charles. "Variations on an Overshot Threading." *The Weaver's Journal*, Fall 1987.

Lyon, Nancy. "Crackle Weave." *Shuttle Spindle & Dyepot*, Winter 1987.

_____. "Crackle Weave, Part II." *Shuttle Spindle & Dyepot*, Spring 1988.
Marston, Ena. "Ways to Weave Overshot: Part I." *Shuttle Spindle & Dyepot*, Fall 1980.

_____. "Ways to Weave Overshot: Part II." *Shuttle Spindle & Dyepot*, Winter 1981.

_____. "Ways to Weave Overshot: Part III." *Shuttle Spindle & Dyepot*, Spring 1981.

Mitchell, Peter. *ABCDraft: A Manual for Drafting and Weaving.* West Newton, Massachusetts: Chesebro-Mitchell Associates, 1992.

Moes, Dini. "Crackle Weave." *Shuttle Spindle & Dyepot*, Winter 1993.

Morgenstern, Marvin M. "Whig Rose Study." *The Weaver's Journal*, Fall 1982.

_____. "Whig Rose Study (continued)." *The Weaver's Journal*, Winter 1982-1983.

Scorgie, Jean. *Weaver's Craft*, Issue 28 – Swivel, Petit Point, & Related Laces, April 2011.

Smith, Mimi. "Treadling and Tie-up Variations for Crackle." *Complex Weavers Journal*, September 2003.

Snyder, Mary E. *The Crackle Weave.* Avon, Connecticut: Book Barn, 1961.

_____. "Crackle Weave and Its Possible Variations." *Handweaver & Craftsman*, Winter 1962.

_____. "Crackle Weave." *The Tie-Up*, newsletter of the Southern California Handweavers' Guild 32, 1982.

Thorpe, Heather G. *A Handweaver's Workbook.* New York: Macmillan, 1956.

Tidball, Harriet. *The Weaver's Book: Fundamentals of Handweaving.* New York: Macmillan, 1961.

Tod, Osma Gallinger. *The Joy of Handweaving.* New York: Bonanza Books, 1964.

Wilson, Susan. "Polychrome Crackle." *Handwoven,* September/October 1994.

_____. "Crackle Weave." *Shuttle Spindle & Dyepot,* Winter 2001.

_____. "Color-and-Weave Effects on Crackle." *Complex Weavers Journal,* October 2008.

Windeknecht, Margaret B. *Creative Overshot,* Shuttle Craft Guild Monograph 31, 1978.

Zielinski, S.A. *Contemporary Approach to Traditional Weaves: Crackle, M's&O's and Others,* Master Weaver Library Volume 8. L'Islet, Québec, Canada: Nilus Leclerc, Inc., 1981.

Multi-Shaft Crackle

Barrett, Clotilde. "Multiple Harness Crackle." *The Weaver's Journal,* July 1979.

Griswold, Ralph E. "Crackle Weave, Part 1: Designing with Blocks and Motifs." 2004. http://www.cs.arizona.edu/patterns/weaving/webdocs.

_____. "Crackle Weave, Part 2: Tie-ups and Treadlings." 2004. http://www.cs.arizona.edu/patterns/weaving/webdocs.

_____. "Crackle Weave, Part 3: Path Design." 2004. http://www.cs.arizona.edu/patterns/weaving/webdocs.

Hutchison, Jean and Caryl Sedushak *Let's Tackle Crackle.* Self-published, 1999.

Laughlin, Mary Elizabeth. *More Than Four.* West Sacramento, California: Laughlin Enterprises, 1976.

Shelp, Wanda and Carol Wostenberg. *Eight Shafts: A Place to Begin.* Worland, Wyoming: Wanda J. Shelp, 1991.

Snyder, Mary E. *The Crackle Weave.* Avon, Connecticut: Book Barn, 1961.

_____. "Crackle Weave and Its Possible Variations." *Handweaver & Craftsman,* Winter 1962.

Strickler, Carol, ed. *A Weaver's Book of 8-Shaft Patterns from the Friends of Handwoven.* Loveland, Colorado: Interweave Press, 1991.

Wilson, Susan. "Designing with 8-Shaft Crackle." *Weaver's* 27, 1995.

Crackle Patterns and Projects

Atwater, Mary M. *Shuttle-Craft Bulletin.* Cambridge, Massachusetts and Basin, Montana: Shuttle-Craft Guild, 1927-1946. (Whole issues on crackle in August 1936, July 1938, and August 1941).

_____. "Notes on the Crackle Weave." *Practical Weaving Suggestions,* Shelby, North Carolina: Lily Mills, vol.2, date unknown.

_____. *The Crackle Weave: Patterns and Notes Prepared for the Shuttle-Craft Guild.* Basin, Montana: Shuttle-Craft Guild, 1930.

_____. *Mary Meigs Atwater Recipe Book: Patterns for Handweavers.* Salt Lake City, Utah: Wheelwright Press, 1969.

Carr, Veva N. "Bedroom in 'Right and Left' Crackle Weave." *The Handicrafter* 6, c. 1934.

Davison, Marguerite Porter. *A Handweaver's Pattern Book.* Swarthmore, Pennsylvania: Marguerite P. Davison, 1944.

de Atley, Suzanne. "Designing with Crackle." *Handwoven,* September/October 1994.

Dixon, Ann. *The Handweaver's Pattern Directory.* Loveland, Colorado: Interweave Press, 2007.

Douglas, Harriett C. "Drapery Materials – Crackle Weave." *The Shuttle-Craft Bulletin,* April 1947.

Edwards, Tomoe. "Cousin Crackle for 4-block, 4-shaft Scarves." *Handwoven,* May/June 2006.

Harstine, Ruby V. "An Appreciation of Jaemtlandsväev." *The Handicrafter,* January/February 1932.

Johnson, Nellie Sargent. "Designing 'Crackle' Weave Patterns." *Handweaving News,* February 1940.

_____. "'Crackle' Weave 'Trees' Adapted from an Ancient Pattern Book." *Handweaving News,* November 1940.

_____. "Some More 'Crackle' Weave Patterns." *Handweaving News,* May 1941.

_____. "Some Crackle Weave Patterns." *Handweaving News,* April 1943.

_____. "Crackle Weave Patterns." *Handweaving News,* September 1945.

_____. "Designing 'Crackle' Weave Patterns Based on Twill Order." *Handweaving News,* March 1947.

Macomber, Dorothea. "Five Crackle Weave Projects." *Handweaver & Craftsman,* Summer 1958.

Modén-Olsson, Maria. *Jämtlandsdräll,* Ostersund: Jamtslogos Forsaljnings forening, 1955.

Peters, Rupert. "Some Notes on Crackle Weave."*Practical Weaving Suggestions,* Shelby, North Carolina: Lily Mills, vol.2, 1957.

Schnee, Karen. Café Grande Mug Rugs." *Handwoven,* May/June 2006.

Shelp, Wanda and Carol Wostenberg. *Eight Shafts: A Place to Begin.* Worland, Wyoming: Wanda J. Shelp, 1991.

Snyder, Mary E. *The Crackle Weave.* Avon, Connecticut: Book Barn, 1961.

Strickler, Carol, ed. *A Weaver's Book of 8-Shaft Patterns from the Friends of Handwoven.* Loveland, Colorado: Interweave Press, 1991.

Wilson, Susan. "Crackle Lap Robe." *Weaver's* 14, 1991.

_____. "Classic Crackle." *Weaver's* 22, 1993.

_____. "Polychrome Crackle." *Handwoven,* September/October 1994.

_____. "Designing with 8-Shaft Crackle." *Weaver's* 27, 1995.

Index

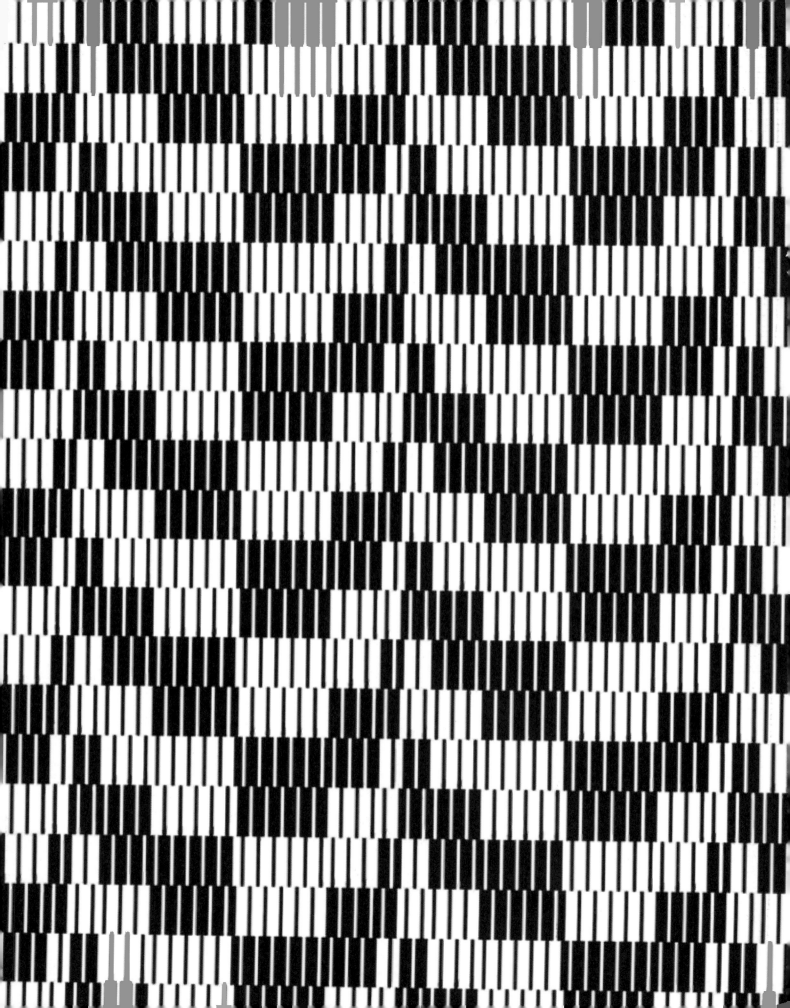